GREAT JAZZ PIANO SOLOS BOOK 2

This publication is not authorised for sale in the United States of America and/or Canada

WISE PUBLICATIONS
part of The Music Sales Group

London/New York/Paris/Sydney/Copenhagen/Berlin/Madrid/Tokyo

Published by
Wise Publications,
14-15 Berners Street, London, W1T 3LJ, UK.

Exclusive distributors:
Music Sales Limited,
Distribution Centre, Newmarket Road, Bury St Edmunds,
Suffolk, IP33 3YB, UK.

Music Sales Pty Limited,
120 Rothschild Avenue, Rosebery,
NSW 2018, Australia.

Order No. AM989164
ISBN 13: 978-1-84609-906-9
This book © Copyright 2007 by Wise Publications,
a division of Music Sales Limited.

Unauthorised reproduction of any part
of this publication by any means including
photocopying is an infringement of copyright.

Compiled by Chris Hussey.
Edited by Jessica Williams.
Arranging and engraving supplied by Camden Music.

Printed in the EU.

www.musicsales.com

Your Guarantee of Quality:
As publishers, we strive to produce every book
to the highest commercial standards.
The book has been carefully designed to make playing
from it a real pleasure. Particular care has been given to
specifying acid-free, neutral-sized paper made from pulps
which have not been elemental chlorine bleached.
This pulp is from farmed sustainable forests
and was produced with special regard for the environment.
Throughout, the printing and binding have been planned to ensure a sturdy,
attractive publication which should give years of enjoyment.
If your copy fails to meet our high standards, please inform us
and we will gladly replace it.

BIRD CAGE WALK JOOLS HOLLAND 50

BLUES ON THE CORNER McCOY TYNER 28

CARAVAN DUKE ELLINGTON 31

CORCOVADO (QUIET NIGHT OF QUIET STARS) ANTONIO CARLOS JOBIM 57

DESAFINADO (SLIGHTLY OUT OF TUNE) ANTONIO CARLOS JOBIM 60

DO NOTHIN' TILL YOU HEAR FROM ME MOSE ALLISON 4

DON'T KNOW WHY NORAH JONES 66

GEORGIA ON MY MIND RAY CHARLES 16

GET YOUR WAY JAMIE CULLUM 24

HONEYSUCKLE ROSE THOMAS 'FATS' WALLER 88

IN YOUR OWN SWEET WAY DAVE BRUBECK 8

LULLABY OF BIRDLAND GEORGE SHEARING 84

MAIDEN VOYAGE HERBIE HANCOCK 44

MAPLE LEAF RAG SCOTT JOPLIN 92

MISTY ERROLL GARNER 41

MONK'S MOOD THELONIOUS MONK 70

NOW HE SINGS, NOW HE SOBS CHICK COREA 18

PERI'S SCOPE BILL EVANS 38

RUBY, MY DEAR THELONIOUS MONK 73

TAKE THE 'A' TRAIN DUKE ELLINGTON 34

YESTERDAYS DUDLEY MOORE 78

MOSE ALLISON
Do Nothin' Till You Hear From Me

Words & Music by Duke Ellington & Sidney Russell

© Copyright 1940 EMI Music Publishing Limited (50%)/Chelsea Music Publishing Company Limited (50%).
All Rights Reserved. International Copyright Secured.

4

D♭9(♯11)
E♭
C7aug5
F9
B♭7
E♭
A♭/B♭
E♭/B♭
Fm7/B♭
E♭
D♭(add 9)
E♭
C♭6/9
E♭
Fm
Gm7
C9
F13
B♭13
B♭7aug5
E♭7
B♭7
E♭7

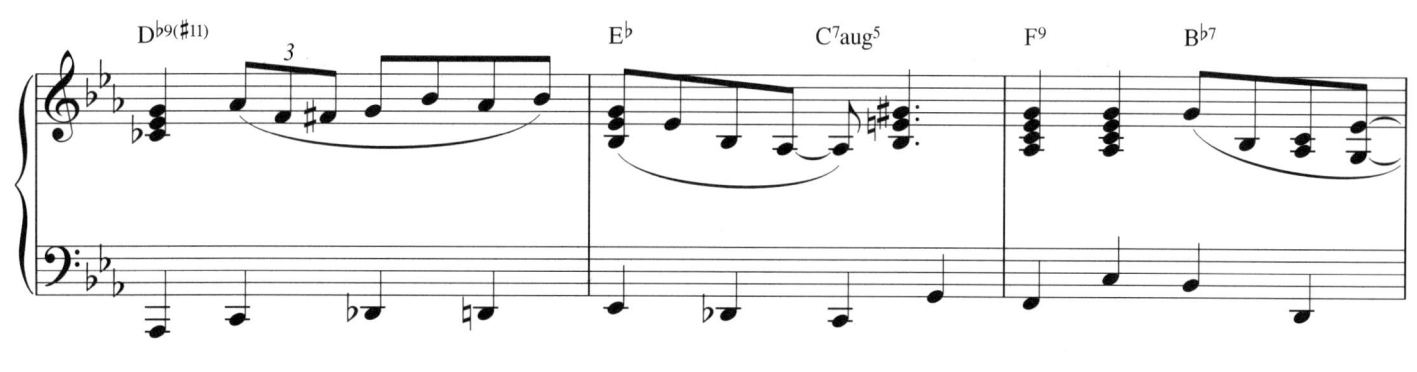

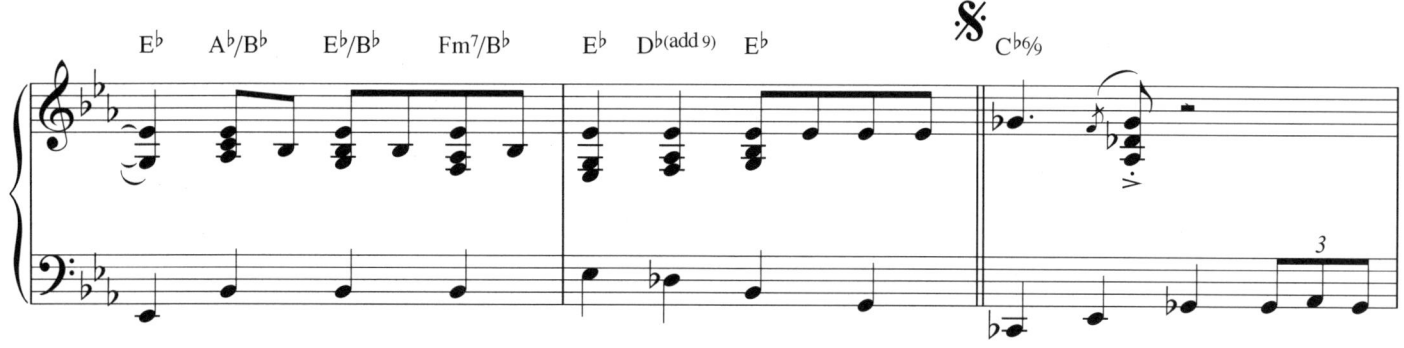

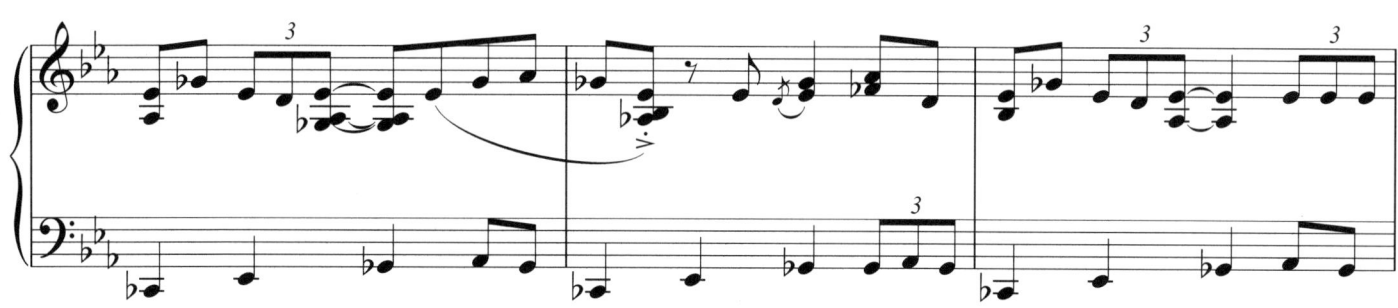

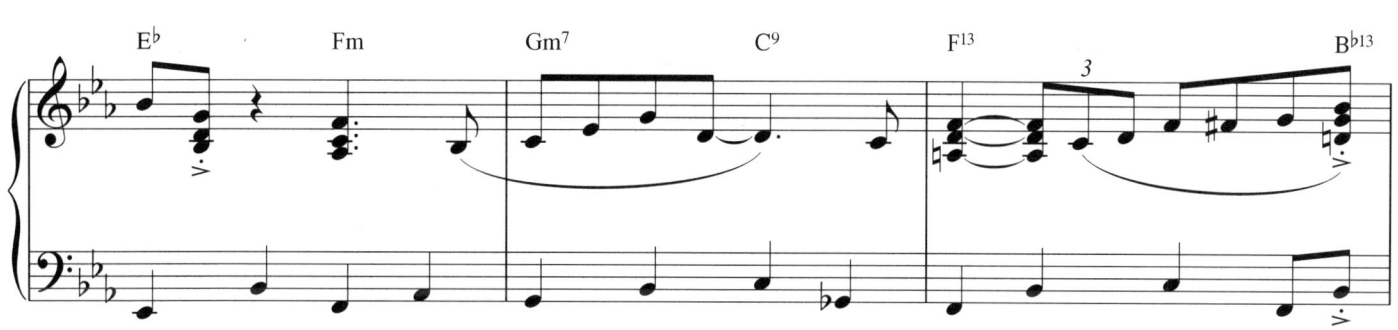

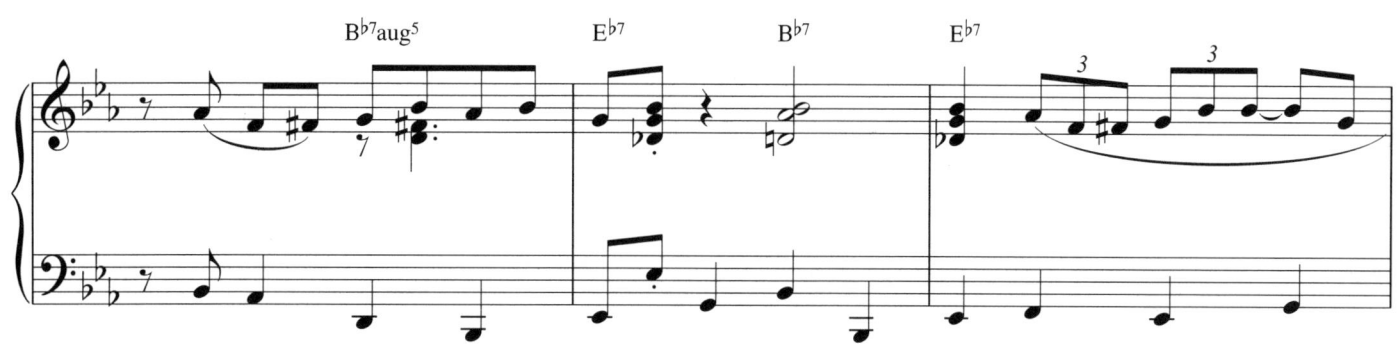

To Coda ⊕

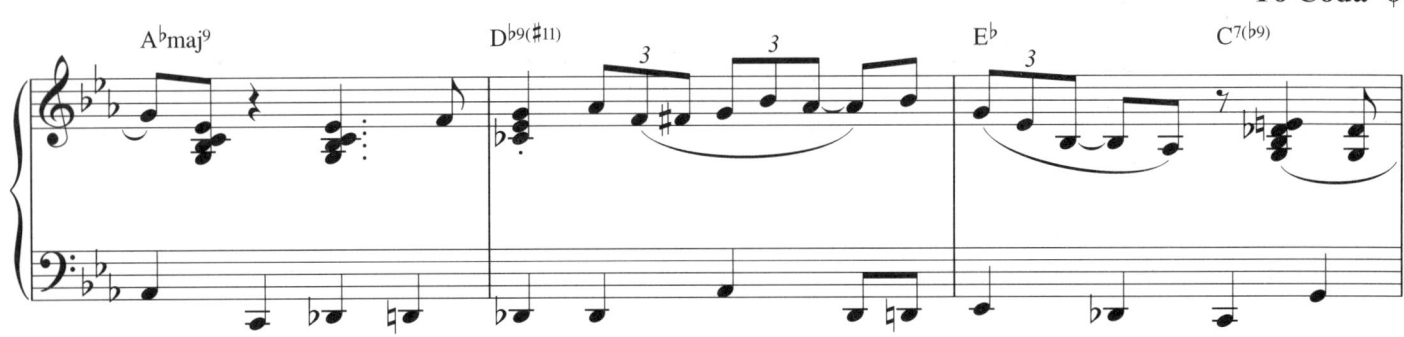
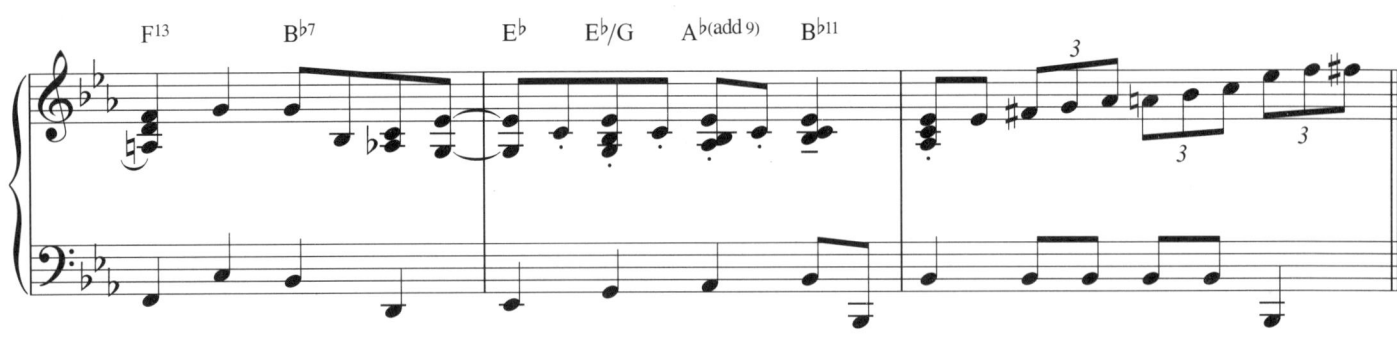

DAVE BRUBECK
In Your Own Sweet Way

Music by Dave Brubeck

© Copyright 1955 Derry Music Company, USA.
Valentine Music Group Limited.
All Rights Reserved. International Copyright Secured.

Moderate

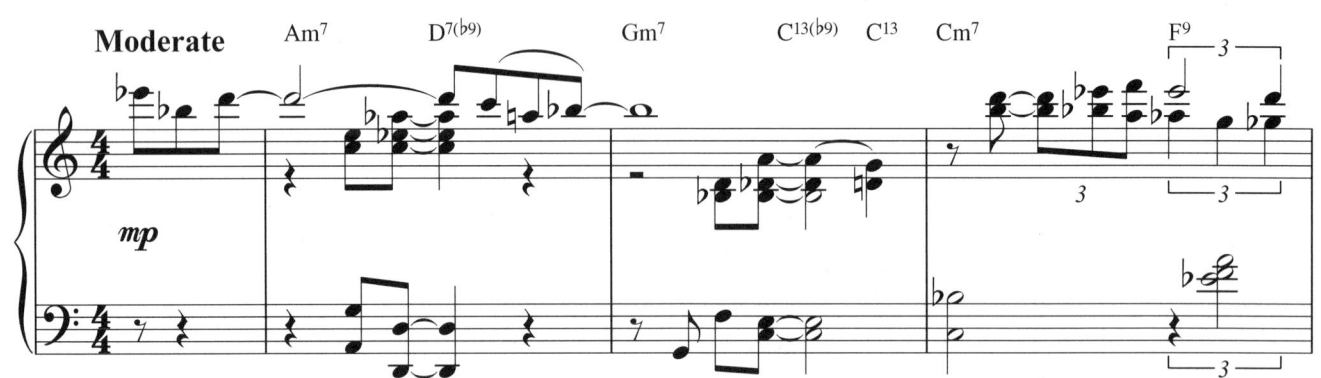

In the style of a waltz

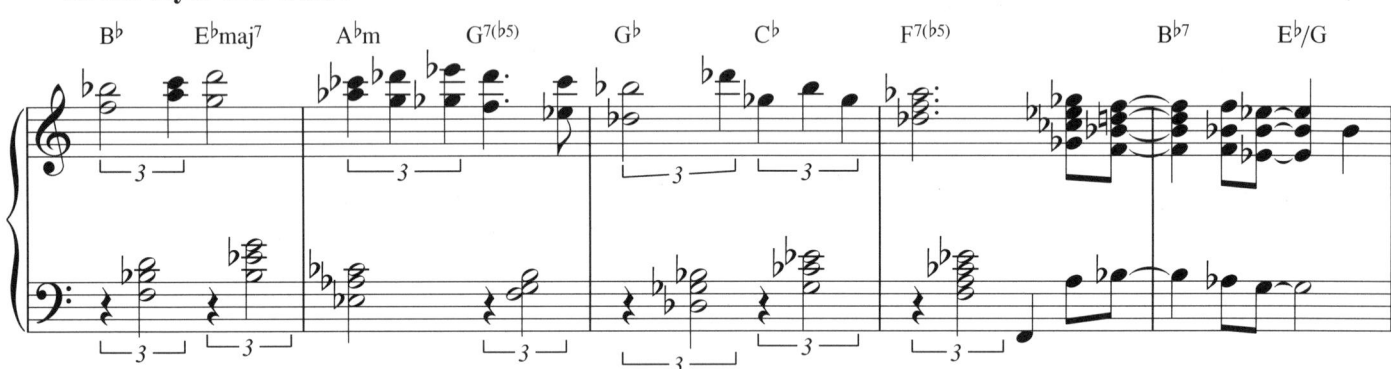

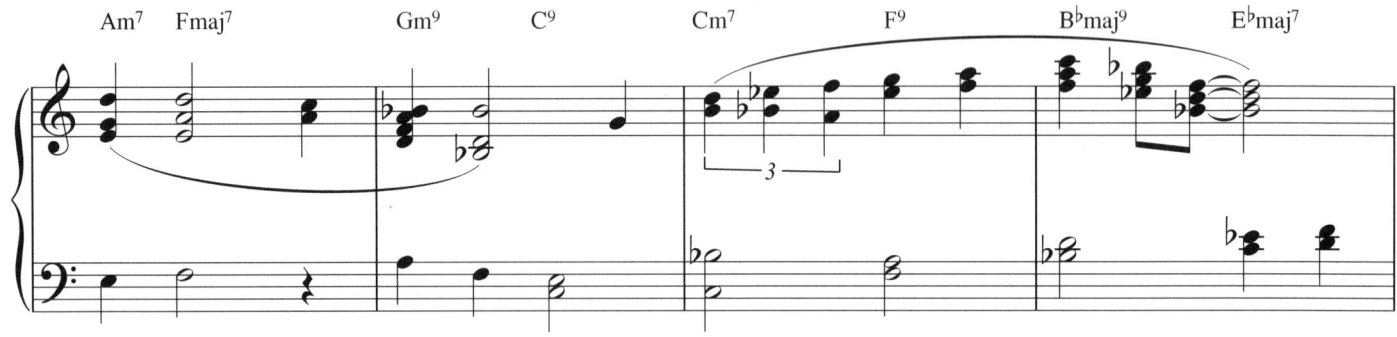

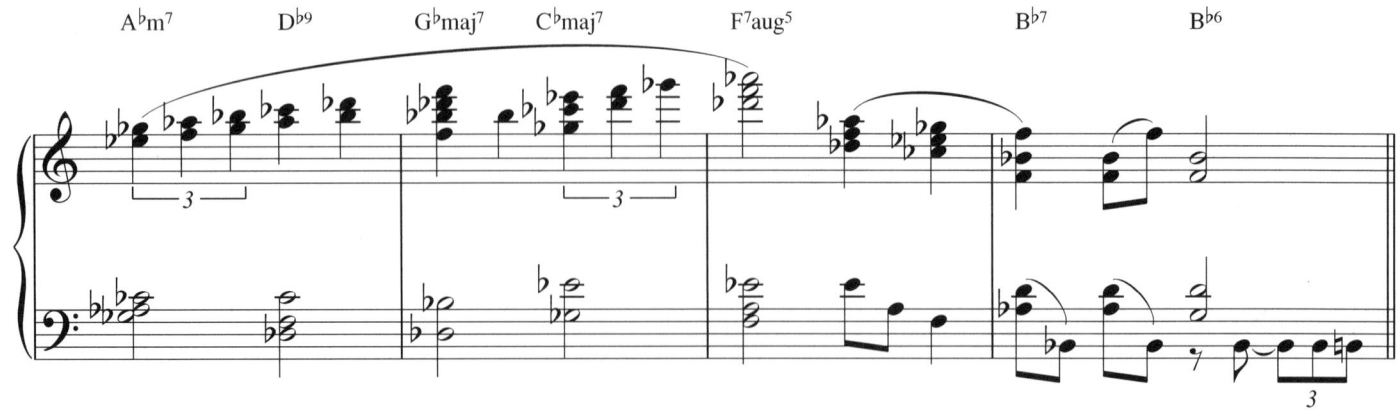

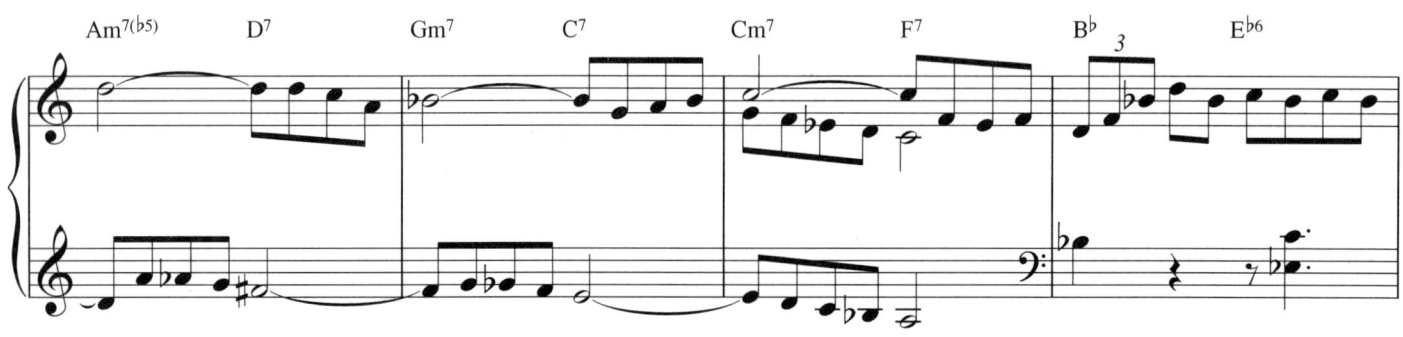
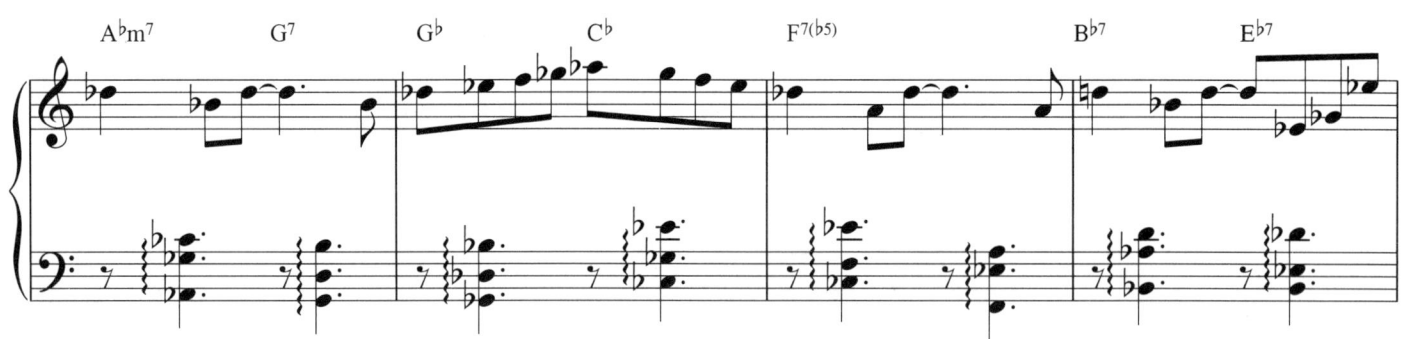
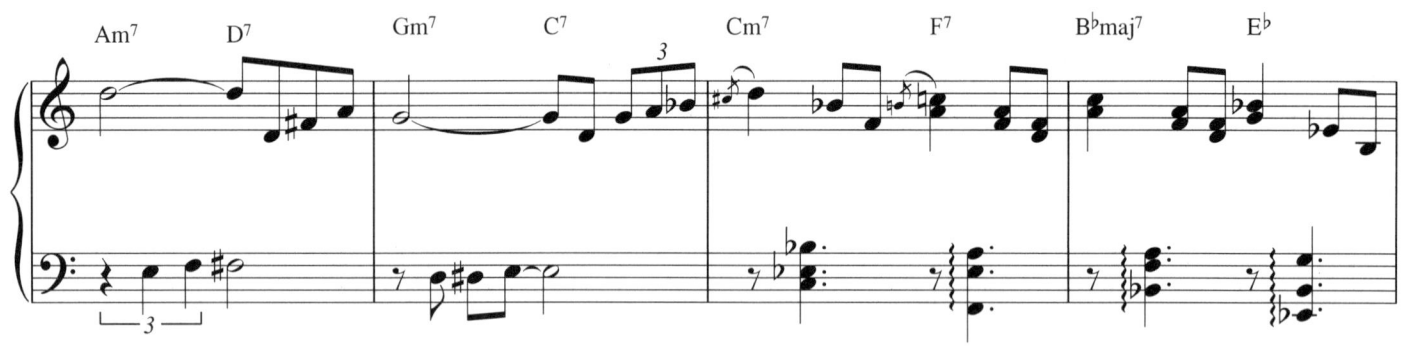

RAY CHARLES
Georgia On My Mind

Words by Stuart Gorrell
Music by Hoagy Carmichael

© Copyright 1930 Southern Music Publishing Company Incorporated, USA.
Campbell Connelly & Company Limited.
All Rights Reserved. International Copyright Secured.

CHICK COREA
Now He Sings, Now He Sobs

Music by Chick Corea

© Copyright 1968 Litha Music Company, USA.
Universal/MCA Music Limited.
All rights in Germany administered by Universal/MCA Music Publ. GmbH.
All Rights Reserved. International Copyright Secured.

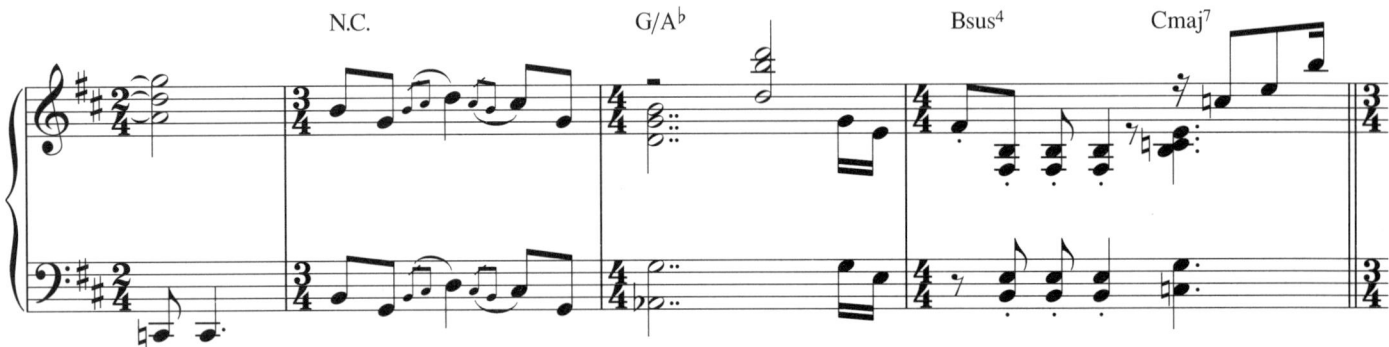

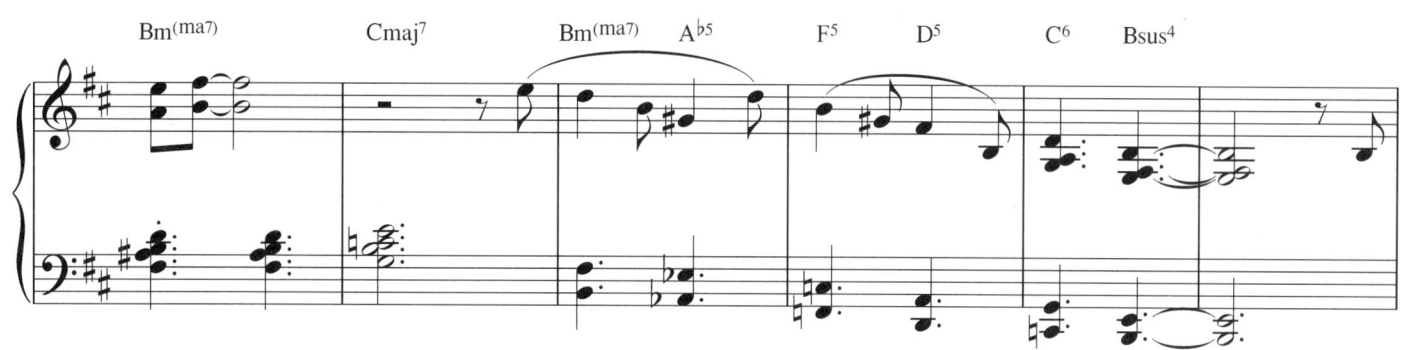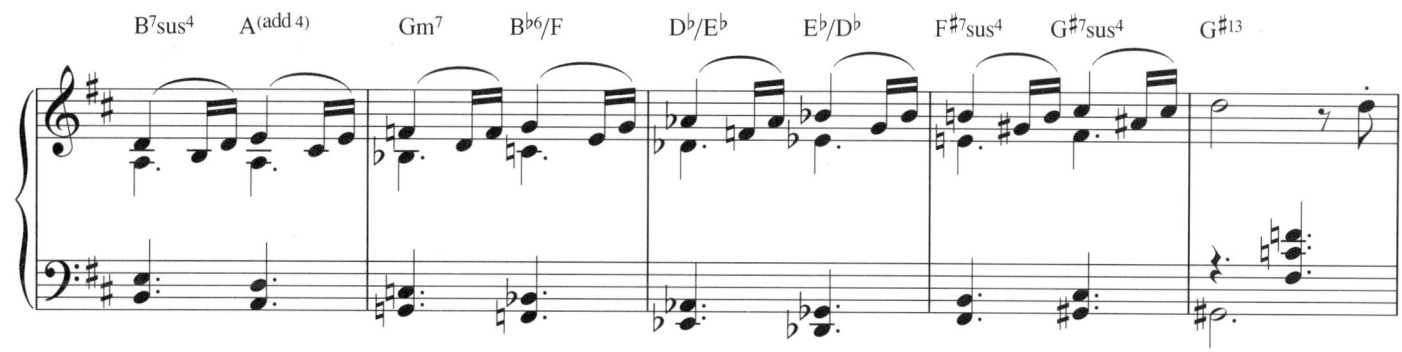

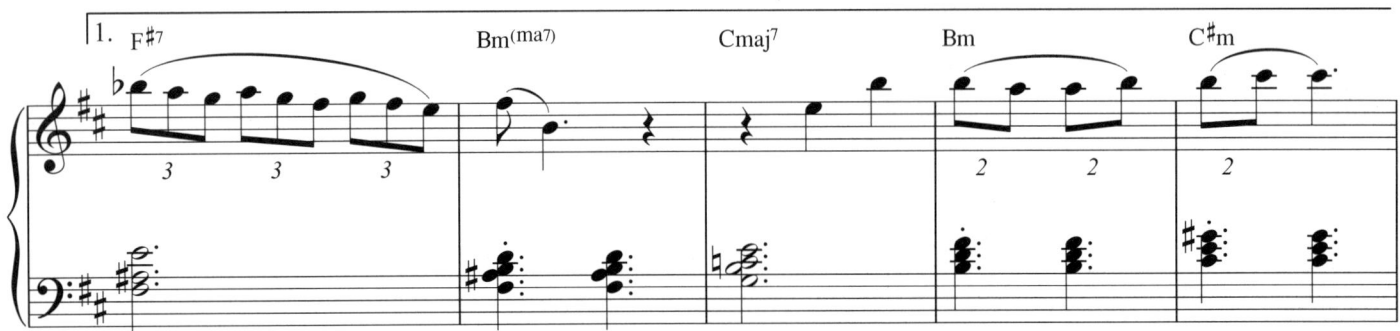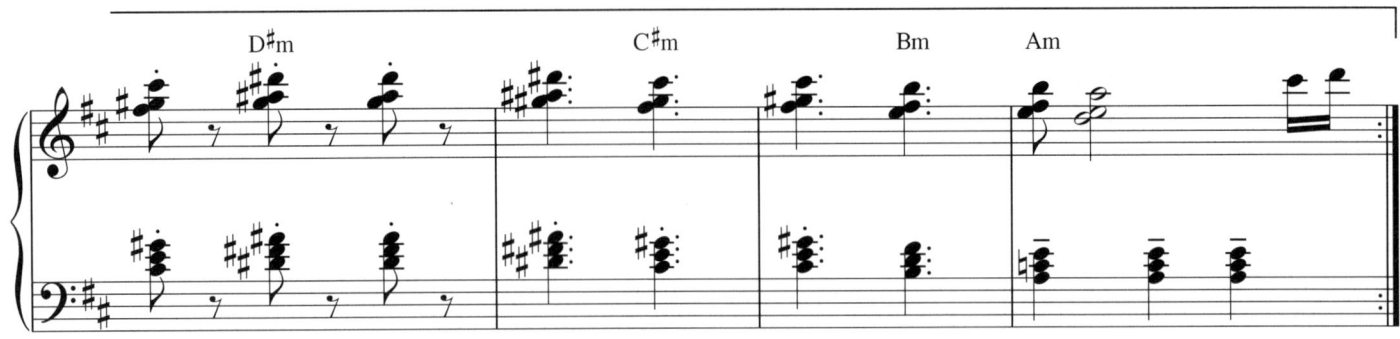

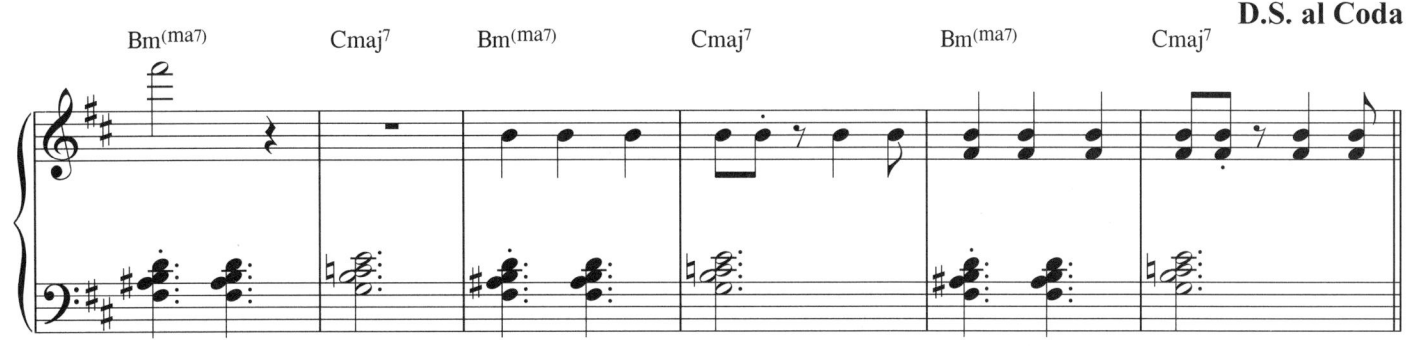

Coda

JAMIE CULLUM
Get Your Way

Words & Music by Allen Toussaint, Jamie Cullum & Daniel Nakamura

© Copyright 2005 Screen Gems-EMI Music Limited (50%)/EMI Music Publishing Limited (25%)/Bucks Music Group Limited (25%).
All Rights Reserved. International Copyright Secured.

Funk Shuffled 16ths ♩ = 90

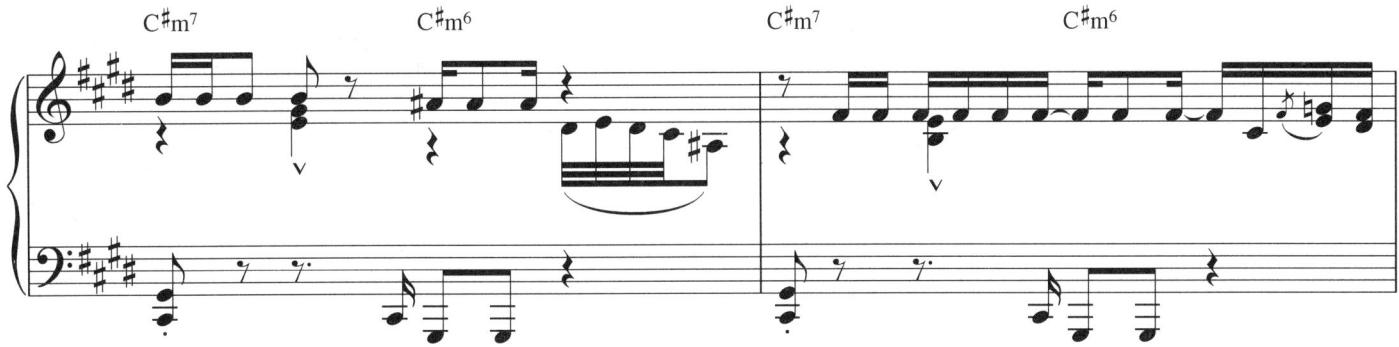
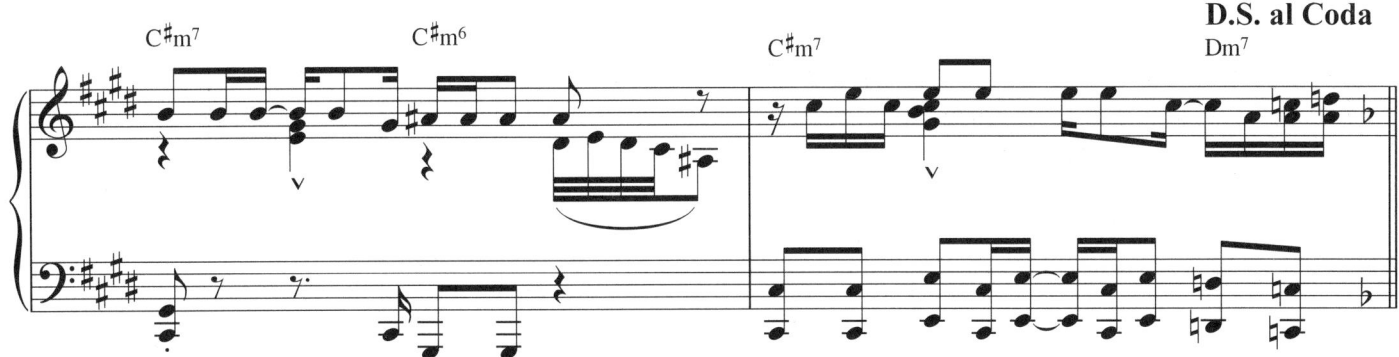

McCOY TYNER
Blues On The Corner

Words & Music by McCoy Tyner

© Copyright 1963 Prestige Music Limited.
All Rights Reserved. International Copyright Secured.

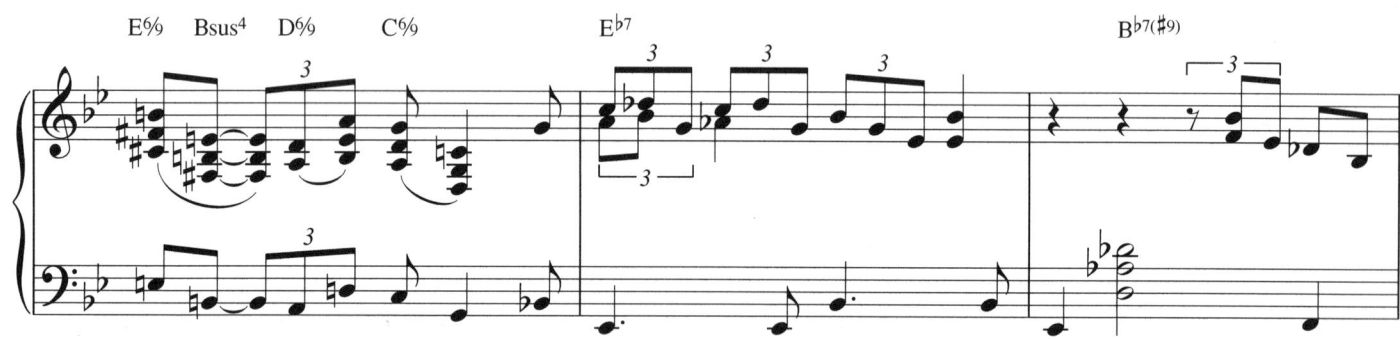

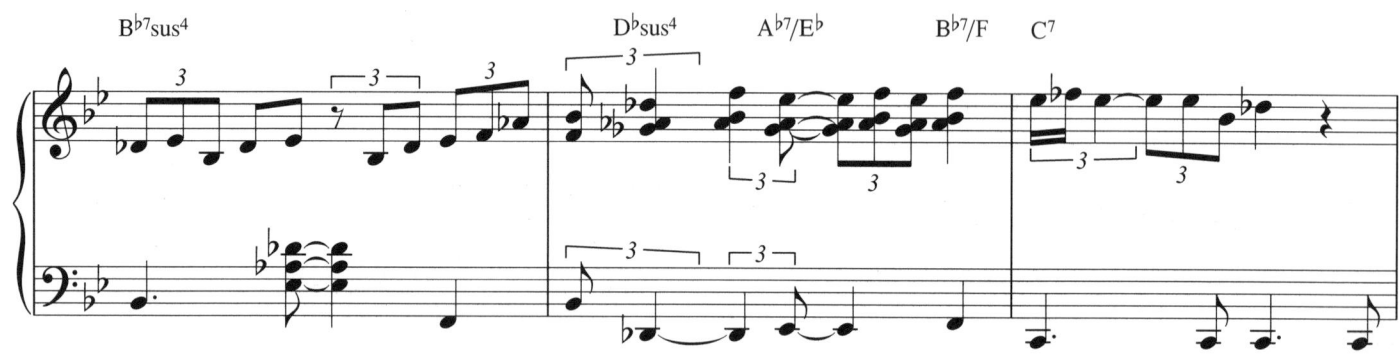

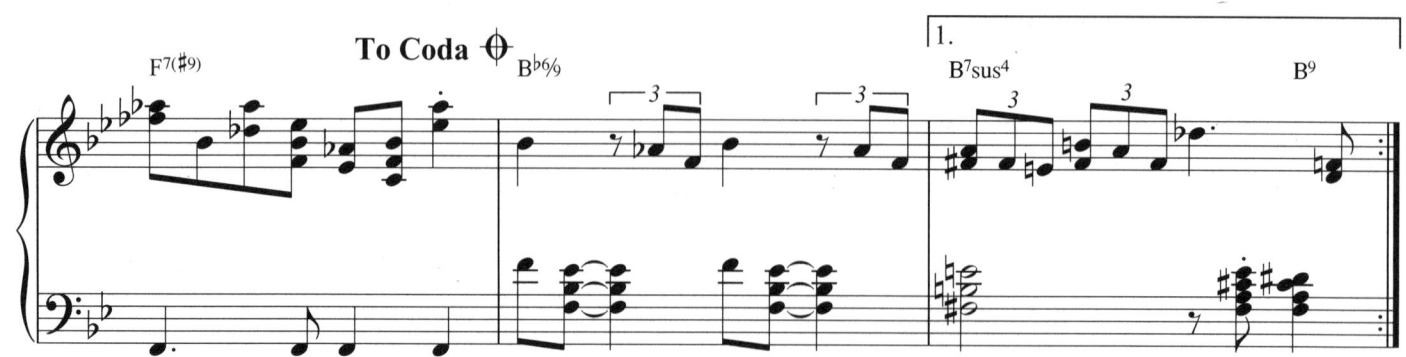

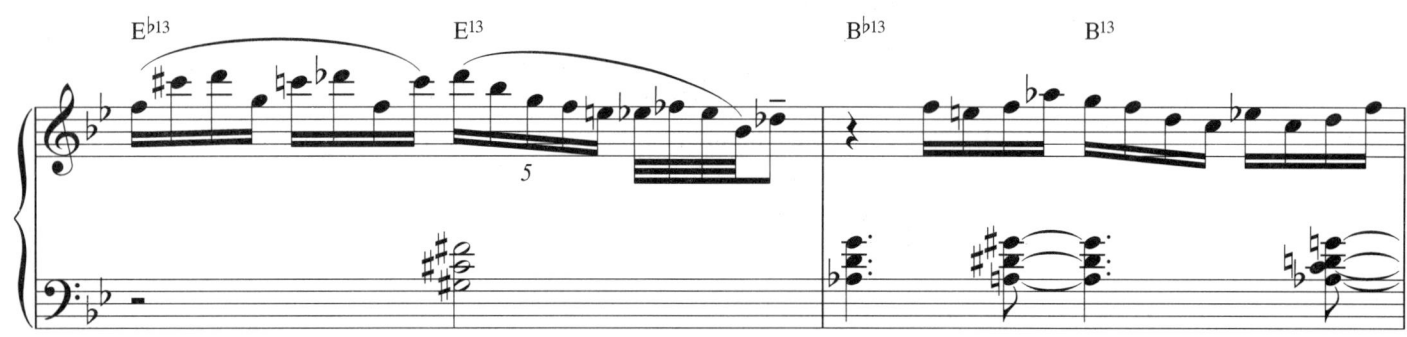

D.S. al Coda

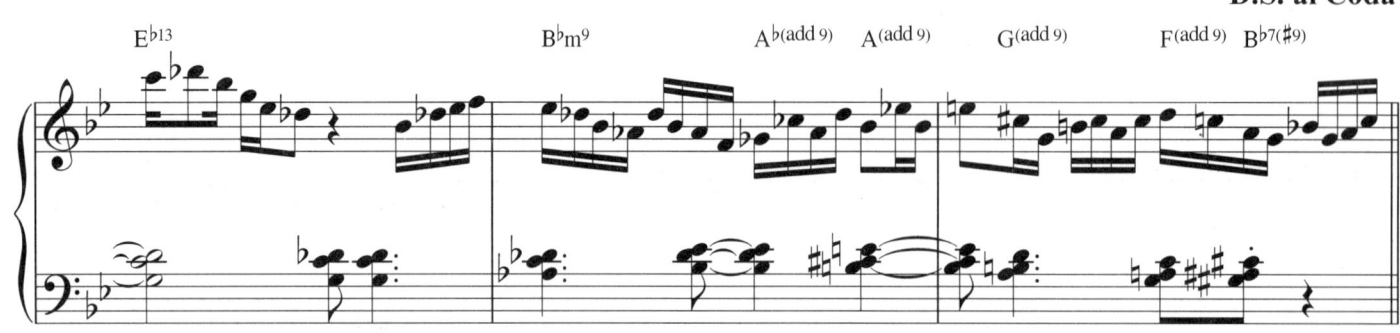

DUKE ELLINGTON
Caravan

Words & Music by Duke Ellington, Irving Mills & Juan Tizol

© Copyright 1937 American Academy of Music Incorporated, USA.
J.R. Lafleur and Son Limited.
All Rights Reserved. International Copyright Secured.

DUKE ELLINGTON
Take The 'A' Train

Words & Music by Billy Strayhorn

© Copyright 1941 Tempo Music Incorporated, USA.
Campbell Connelly & Company Limited.
All Rights Reserved. International Copyright Secured

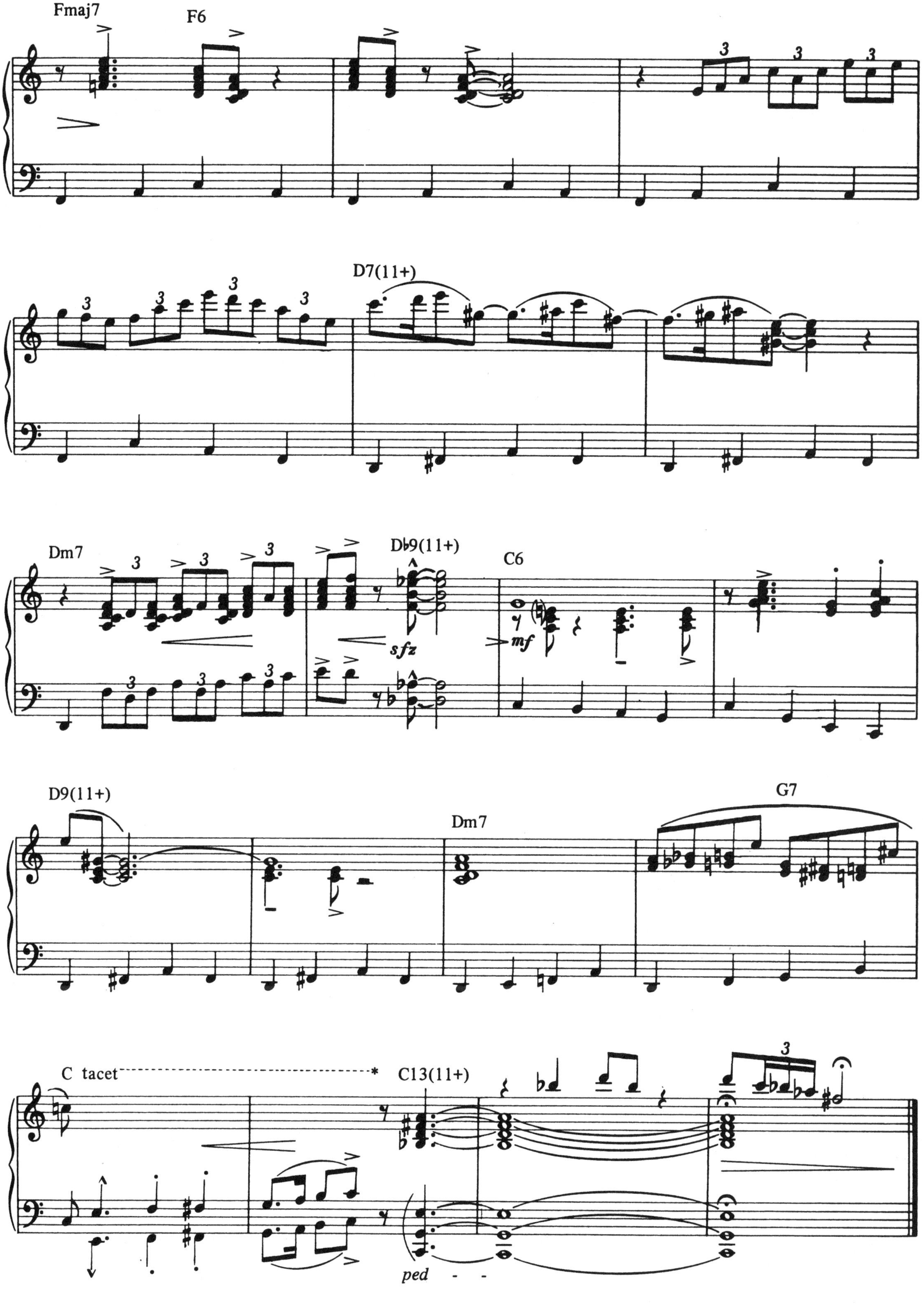
Fmaj7
F6
D7(11+)
Dm7
D♭9(11+)
sfz
C6
mf
D9(11+)
Dm7
G7
C tacet
C13(11+)
ped

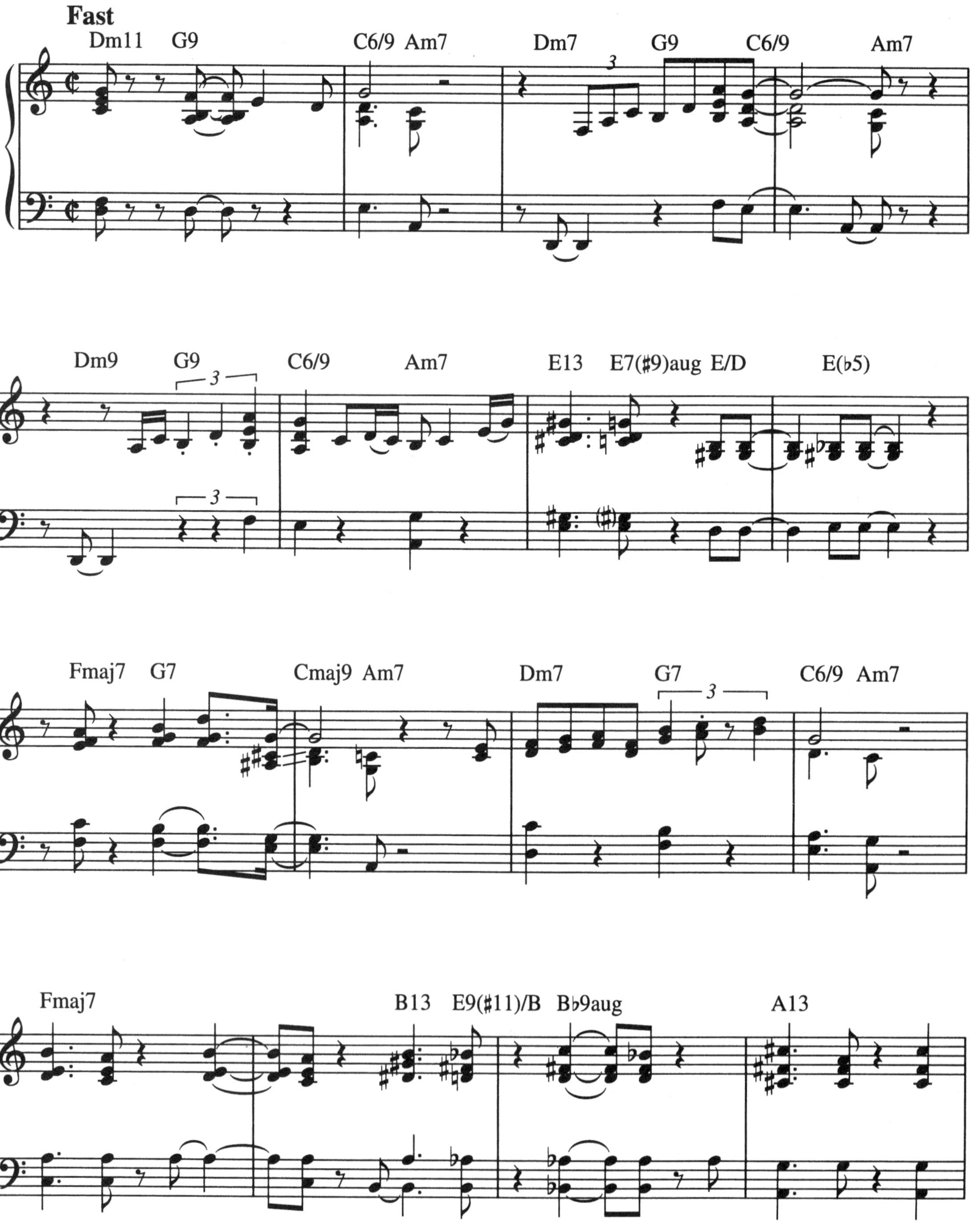

Dm9 G9 C6/9 Am7 Dm9 G13 Em7sus4 A7/E♭ Dm9
Dm7 Dm11/G G13 C6/9 N.C.
Dm11 G13 3 Cmaj9 Am9 Dm9 G13 3 3 Cmaj9 Am9 Dm9
G13 Cmaj9 Am9 E13 E9aug E7 E6(♭5/maj7) E7aug

Fmaj7 G7
C6/9 Am7
Dm7
G7
3
C6/9
Am7
Fmaj7
B13
Gm/F
B♭9aug
A13
Aaug
A13 Dm9
G9
C6/9
Am7
Dm9
G13
Em7add4
A7aug/E♭
Dm9
Dm7
Dm11
G13
C6/9

ERROLL GARNER
Misty

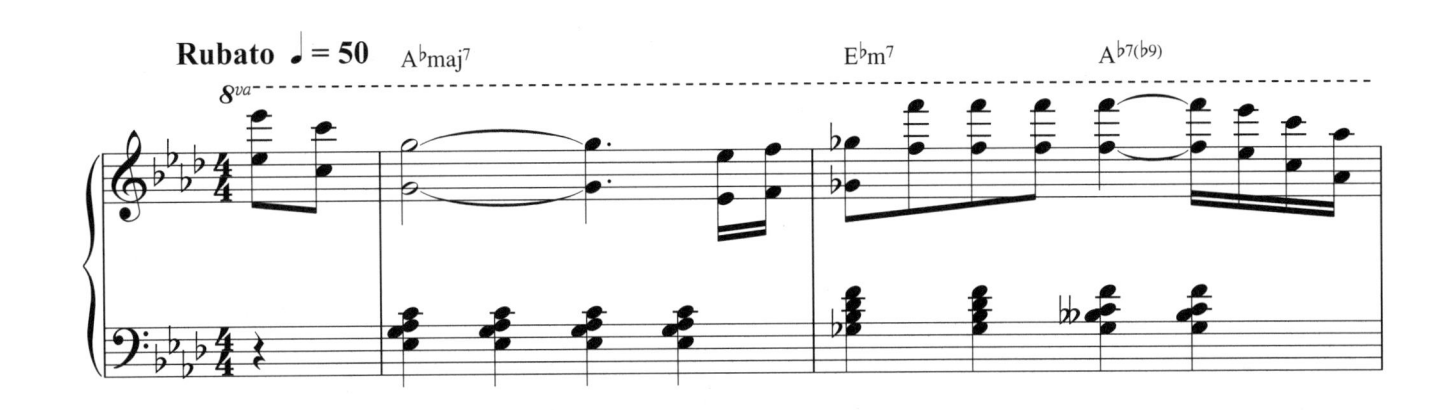

Words & Music by Erroll Garner & Johnny Burke

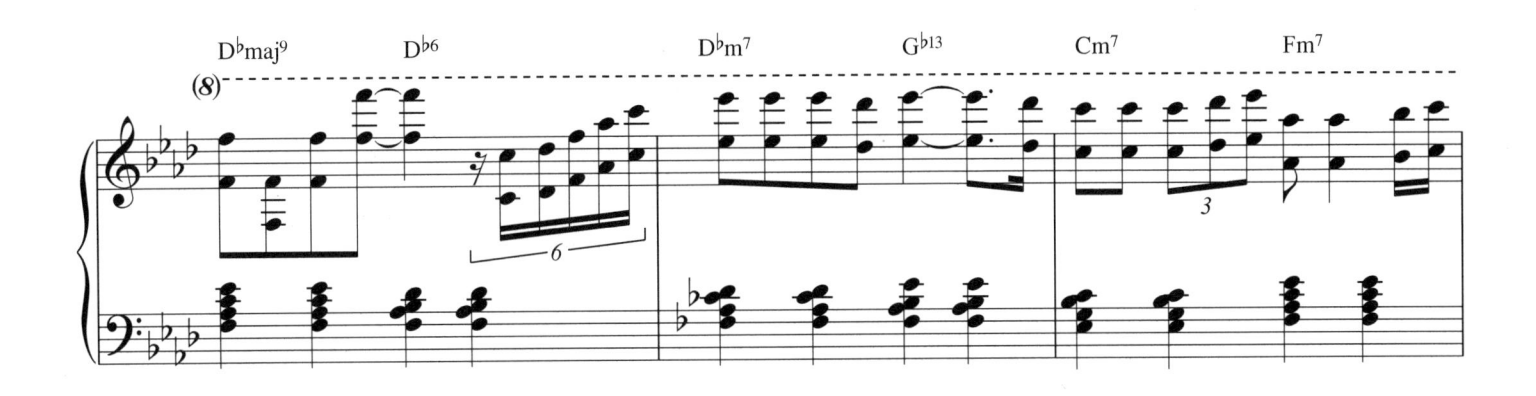

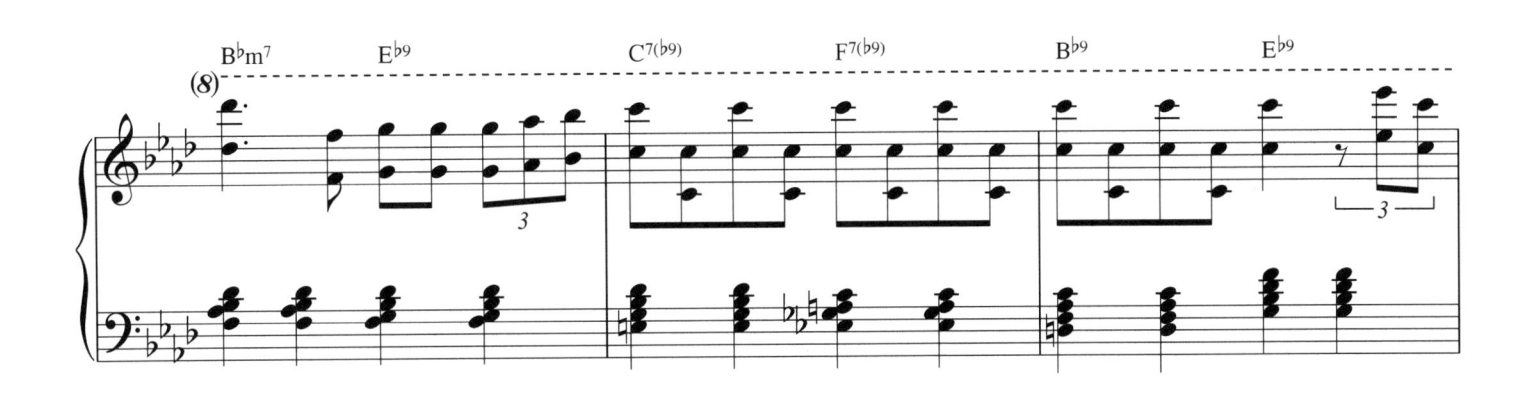

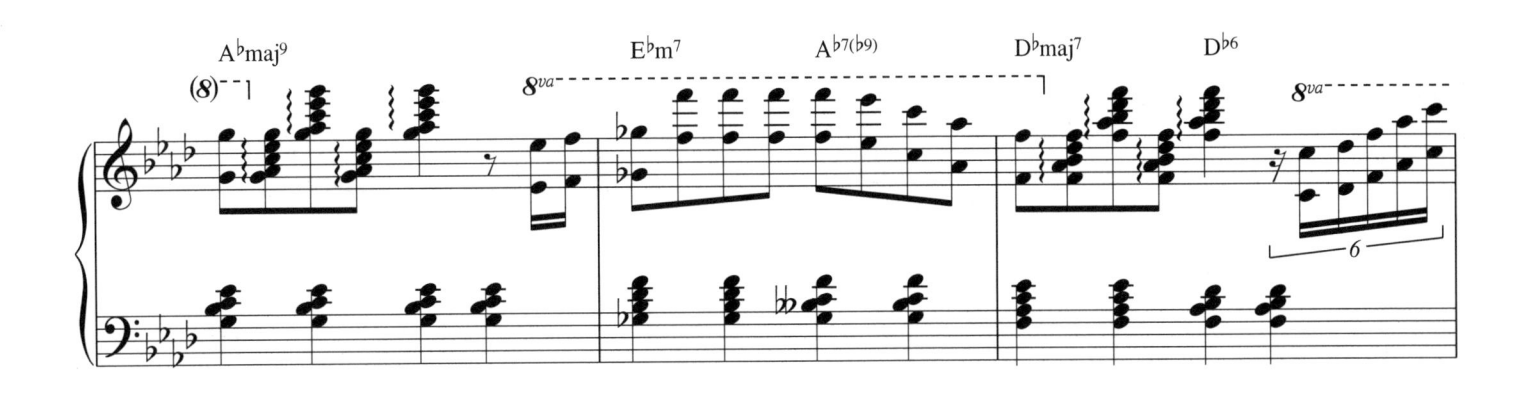

42

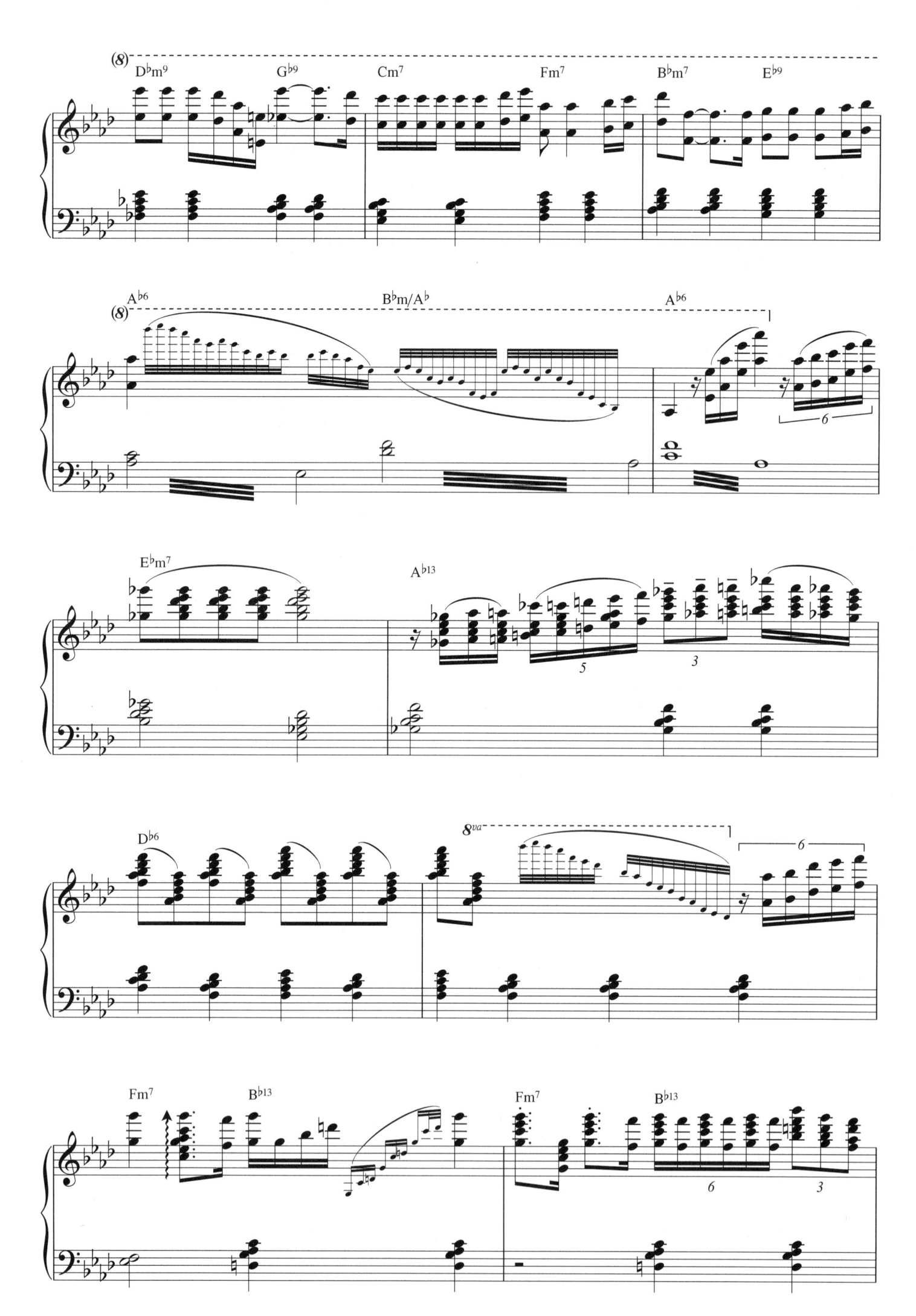

43

HERBIE HANCOCK
Maiden Voyage

Words & Music by Herbie Hancock

© Copyright 1973 Hancock Music Company.
Sony/ATV Music Publishing (UK) Limited.
All Rights Reserved. International Copyright Secured.

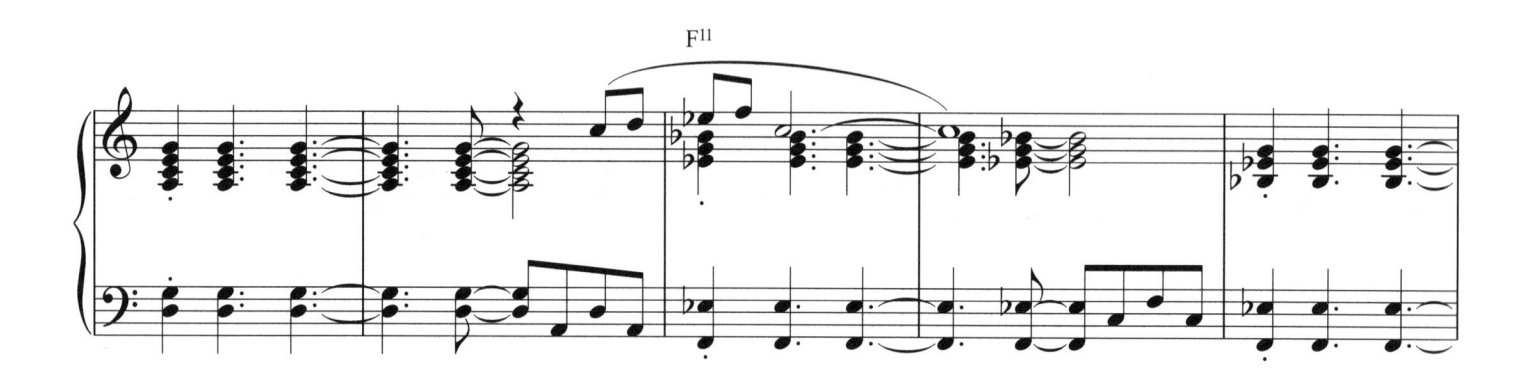

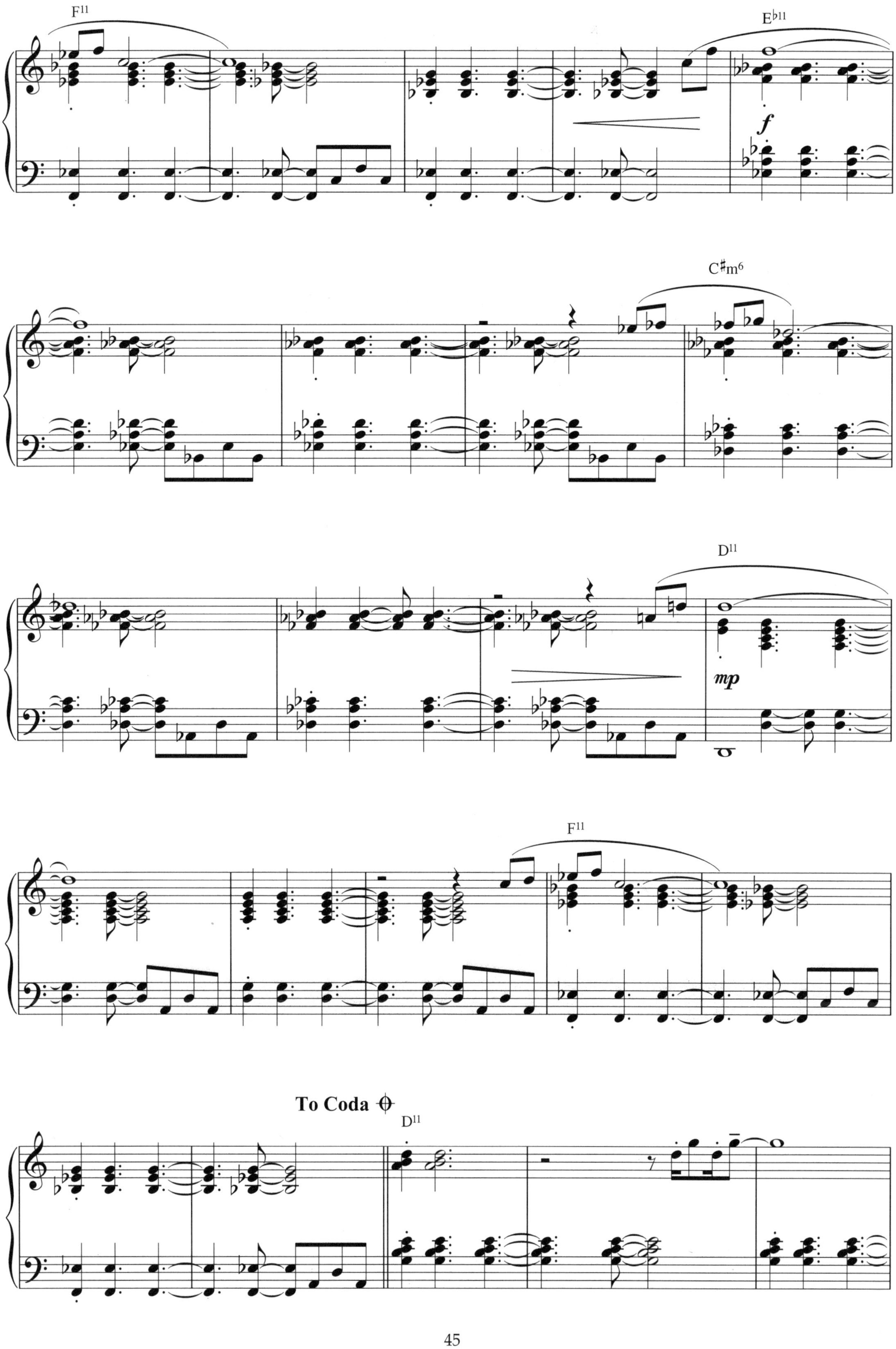
F11
E♭11
C♯m6
D11
F11
To Coda
D11

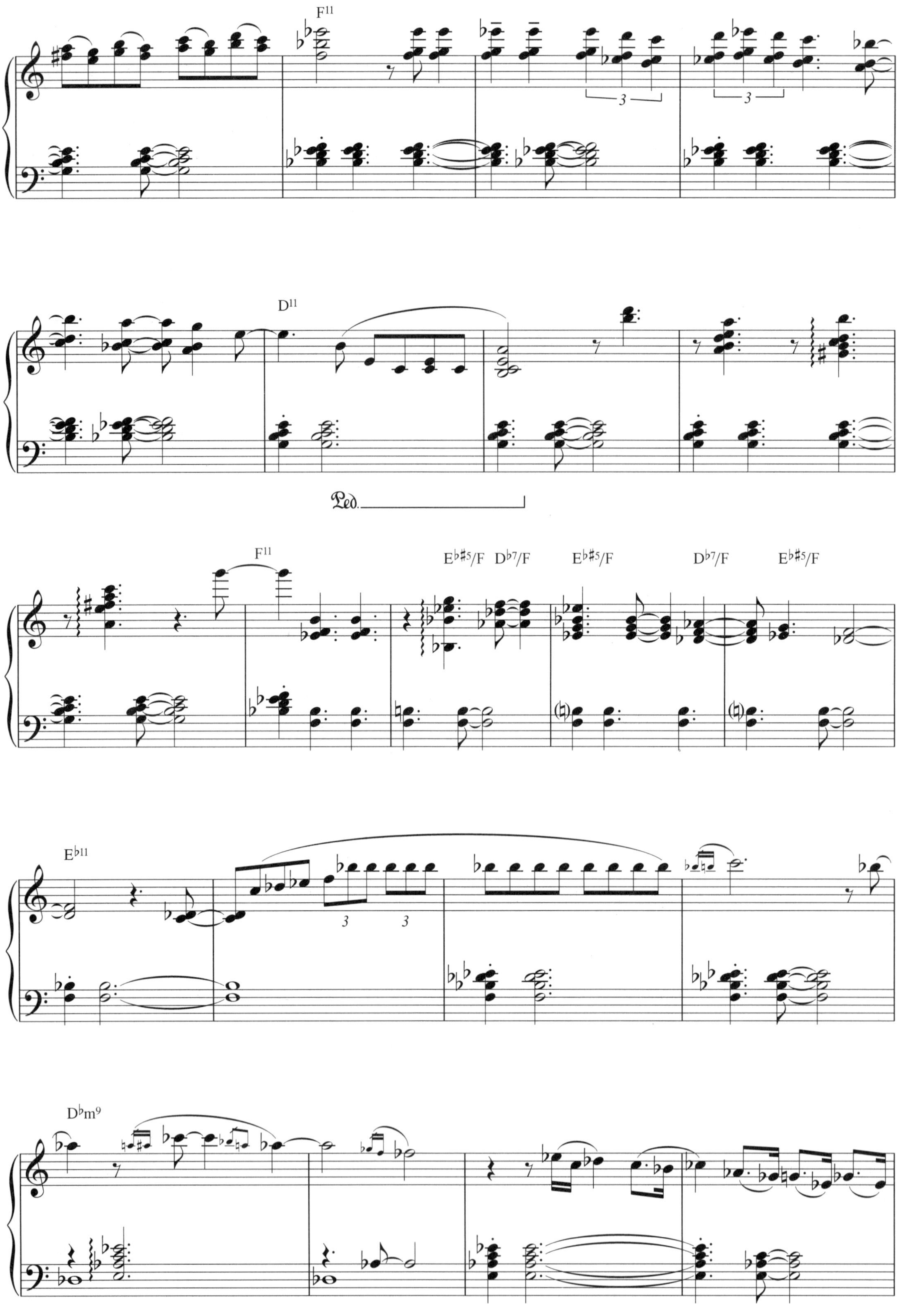
F11
D11
Ped.
F11
E♭♯5/F
D♭7/F
E♭♯5/F
D♭7/F
E♭♯5/F
E♭11
D♭m9

47

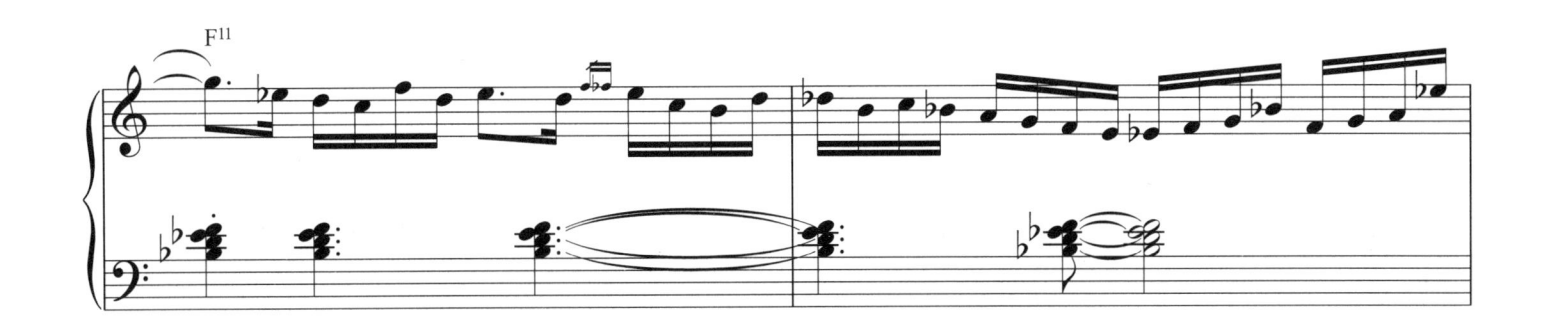

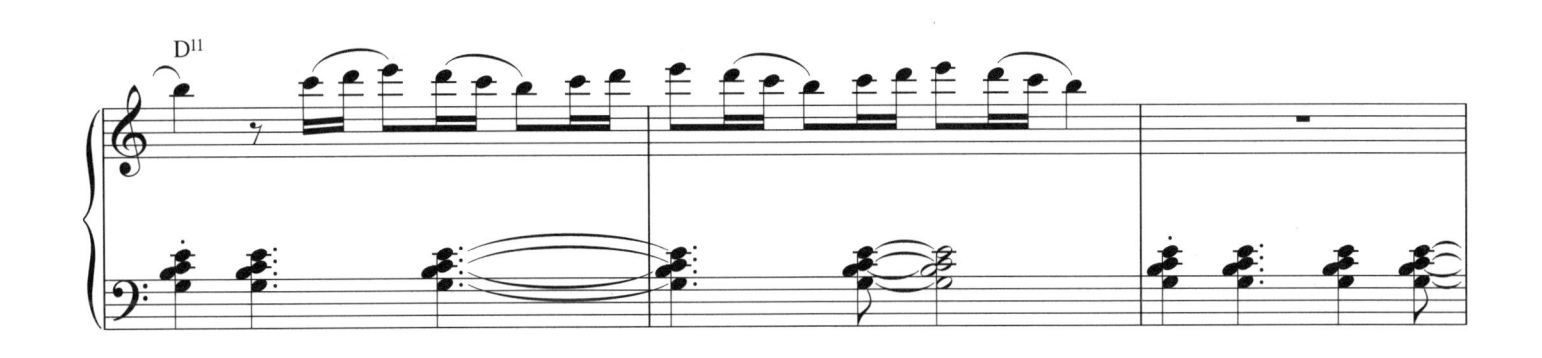

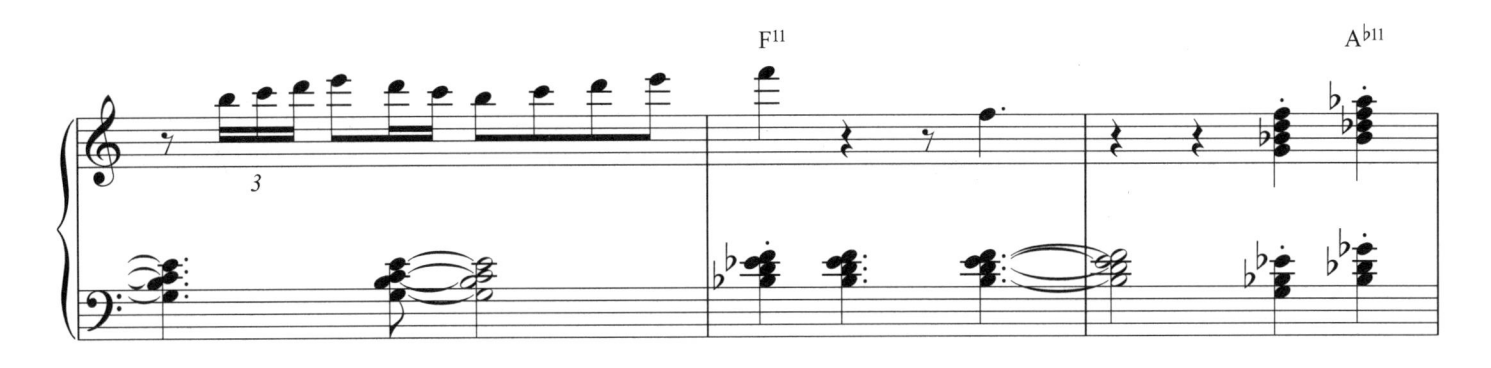

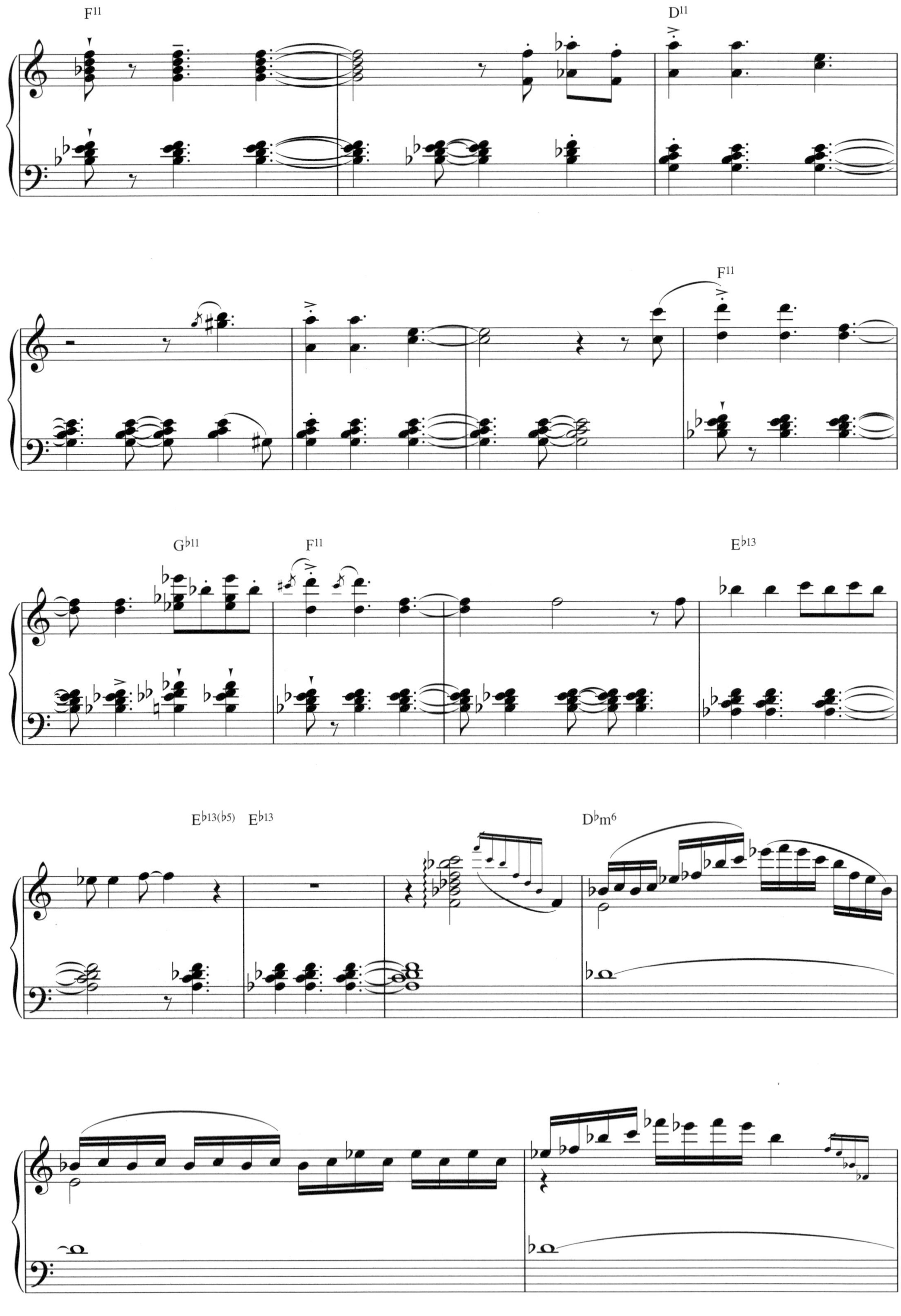
F11
D11
F11
G♭11
F11
E♭13
E♭13(♭5)
E♭13
D♭m6

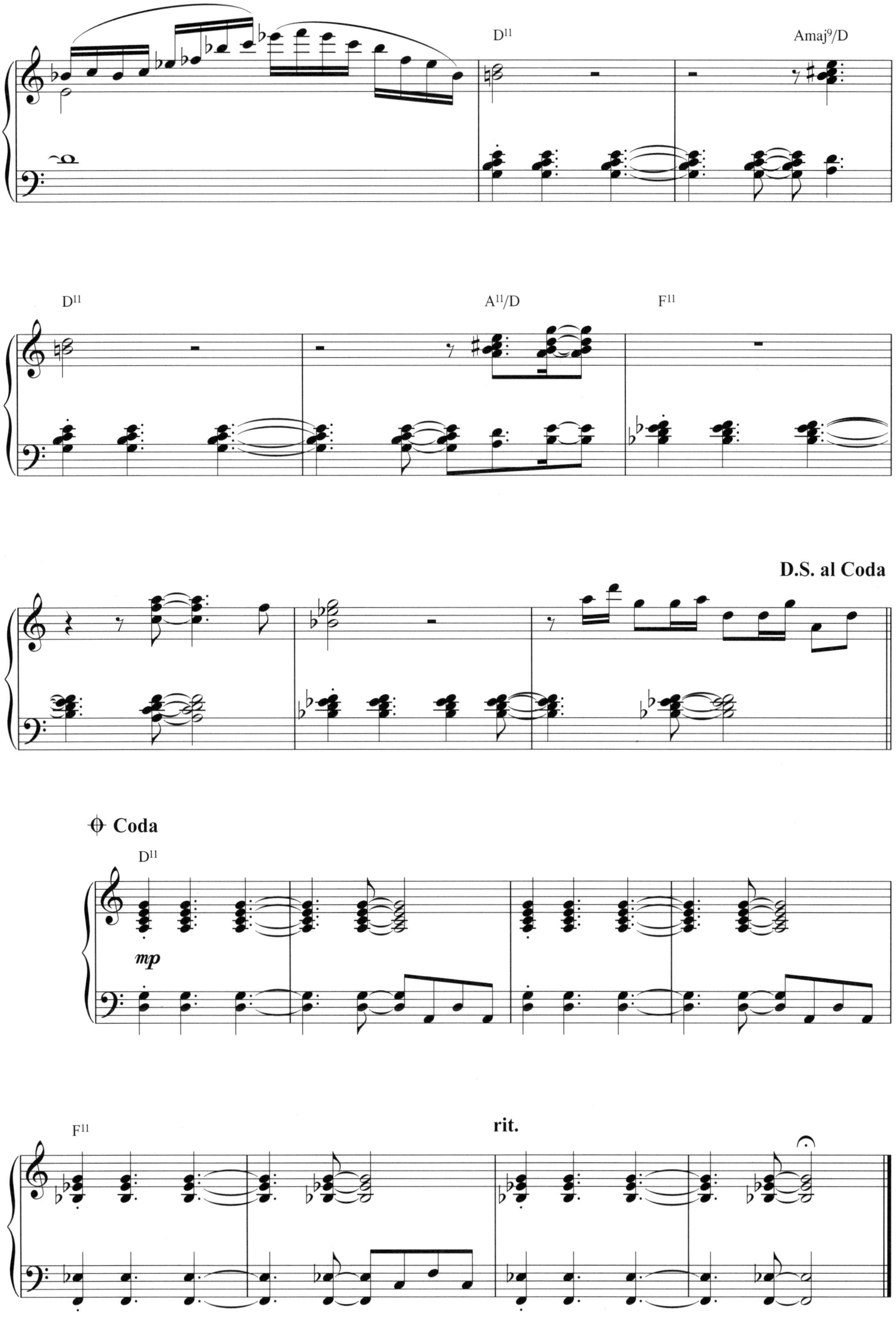
D11
Amaj9/D
D11
A11/D
F11
D.S. al Coda
Coda
D11
mp
F11
rit.

JOOLS HOLLAND
Doing The Bird Cage Walk

Words & Music by Jools Holland & Gilson Lavis

© Copyright 1992 Bugle Songs Limited.
All Rights Reserved. International Copyright Secured.

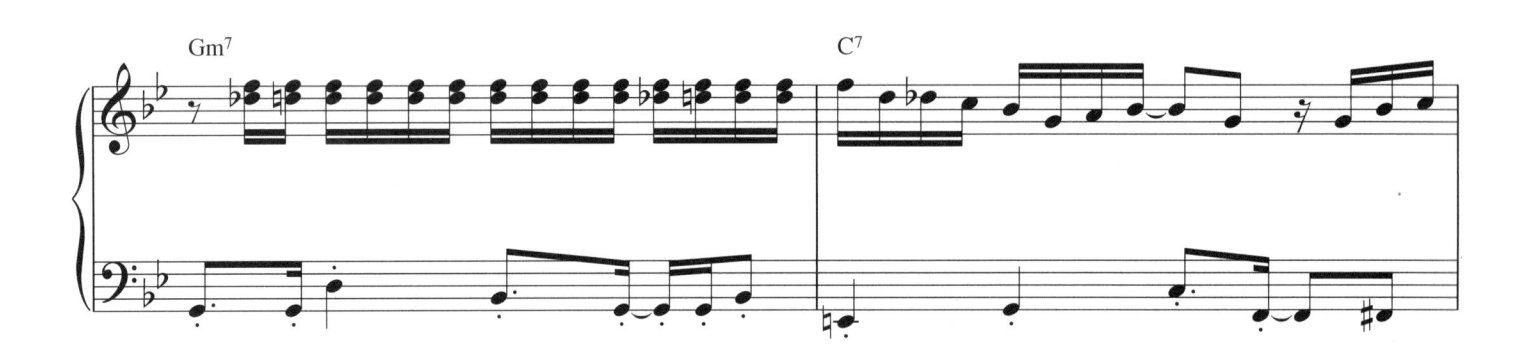

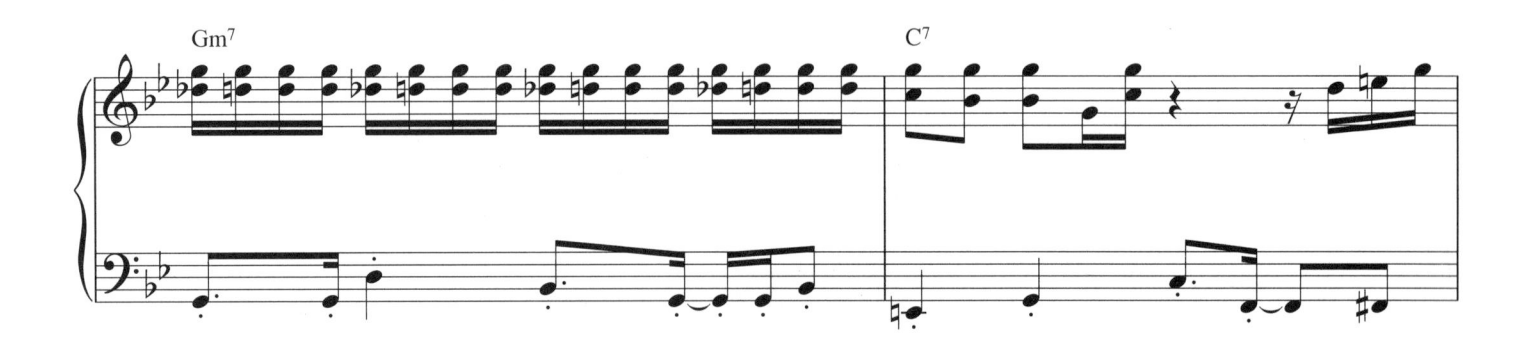

Uptempo Boogie

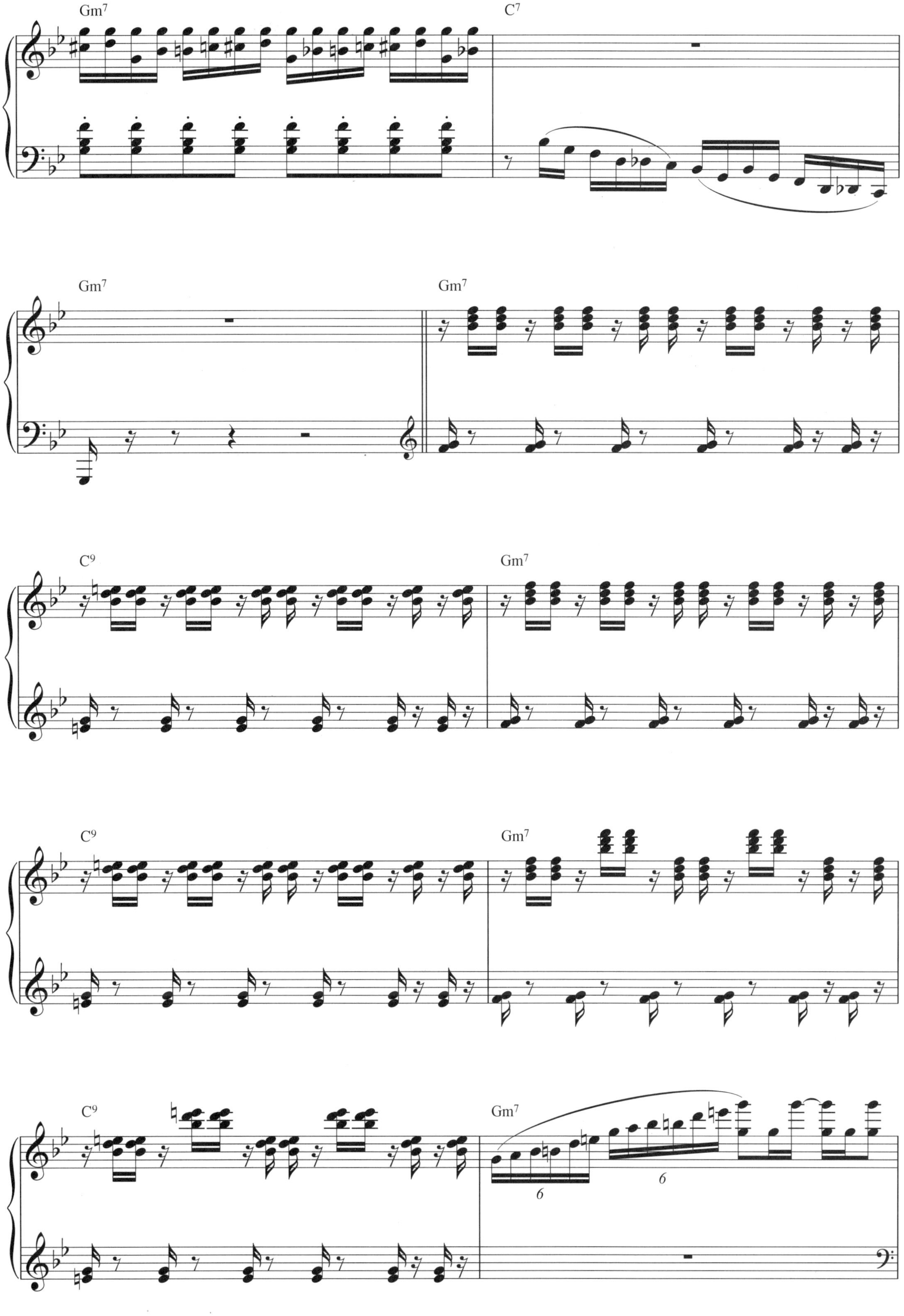
Gm7
C7
Gm7
Gm7
C9
Gm7
C9
Gm7
C9
Gm7
6
6

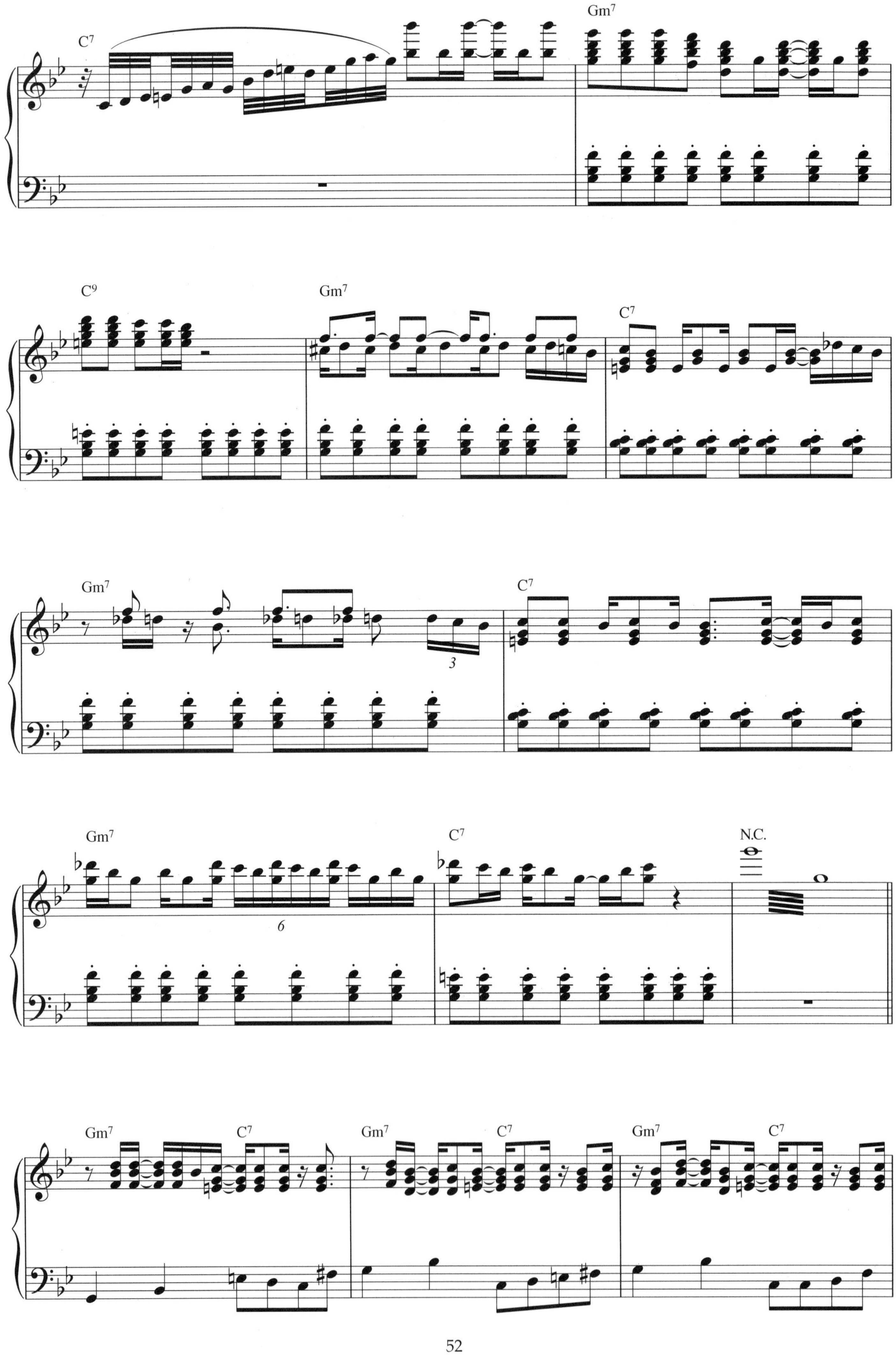
C7
Gm7
C9
Gm7
C7
Gm7
3
C7
Gm7
6
C7
N.C.
Gm7
C7
Gm7
C7
Gm7
C7

Gm7 C7 Gm7 C7 Gm7 C7
Gm7 C7 Gm7 C7 Gm7 C7
Gm7 C7 Gm7 C7 N.C.
Gm7 C7 Gm7
C7 Gm7 C7

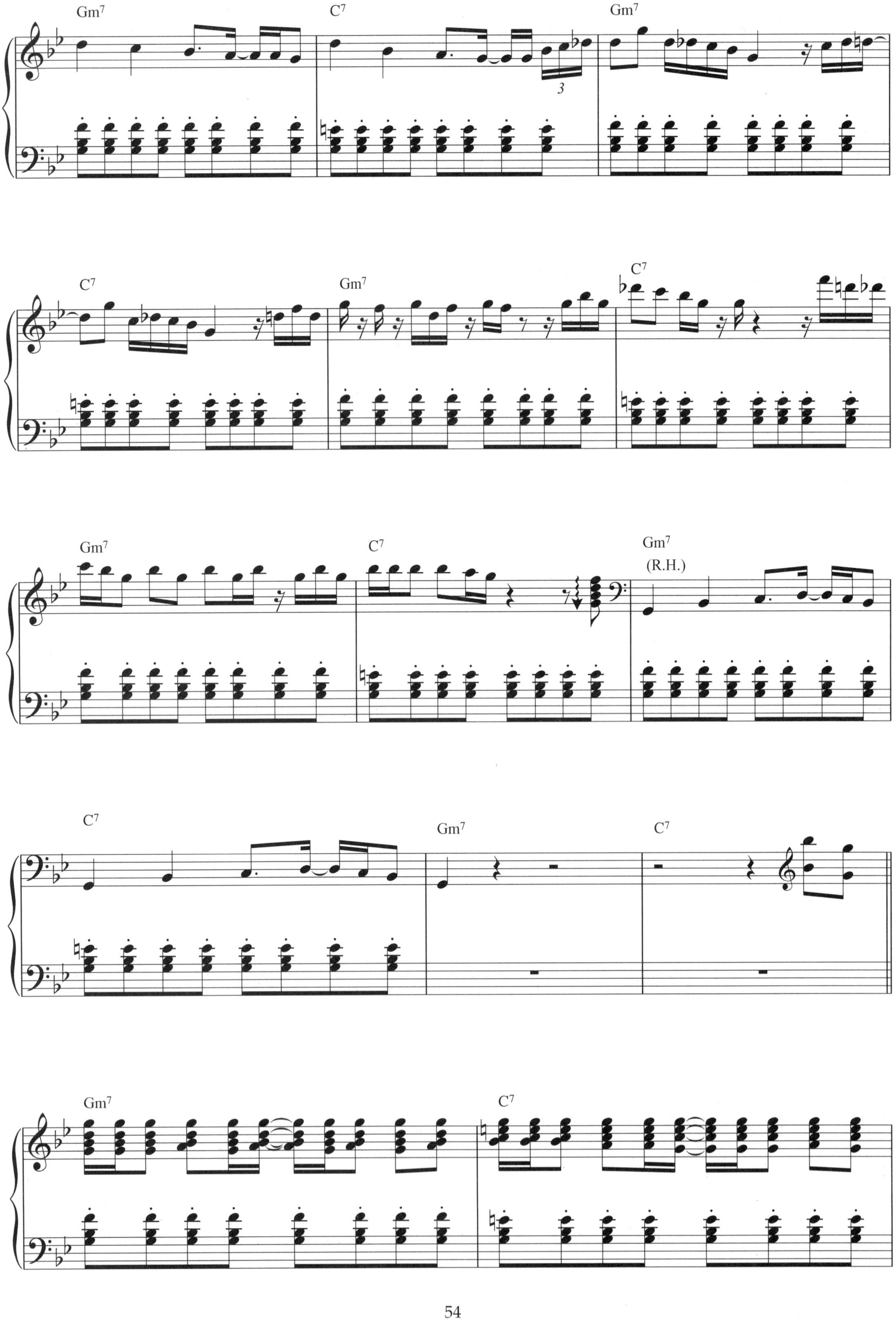
Gm7
C7
Gm7
3
C7
Gm7
C7
Gm7
C7
Gm7
(R.H.)
C7
Gm7
C7
Gm7
C7

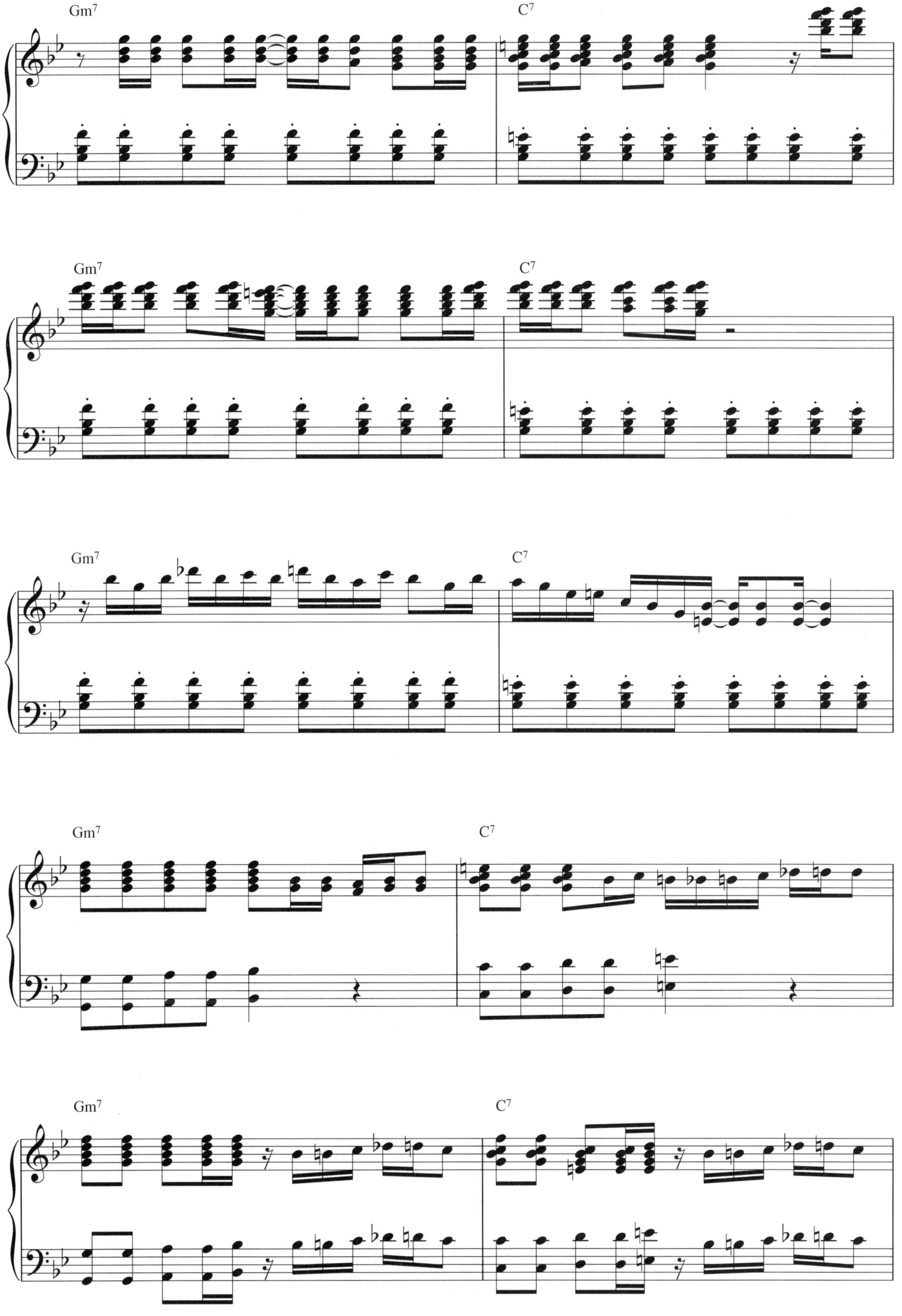
Gm7
C7
Gm7
C7
Gm7
C7
Gm7
C7
Gm7
C7

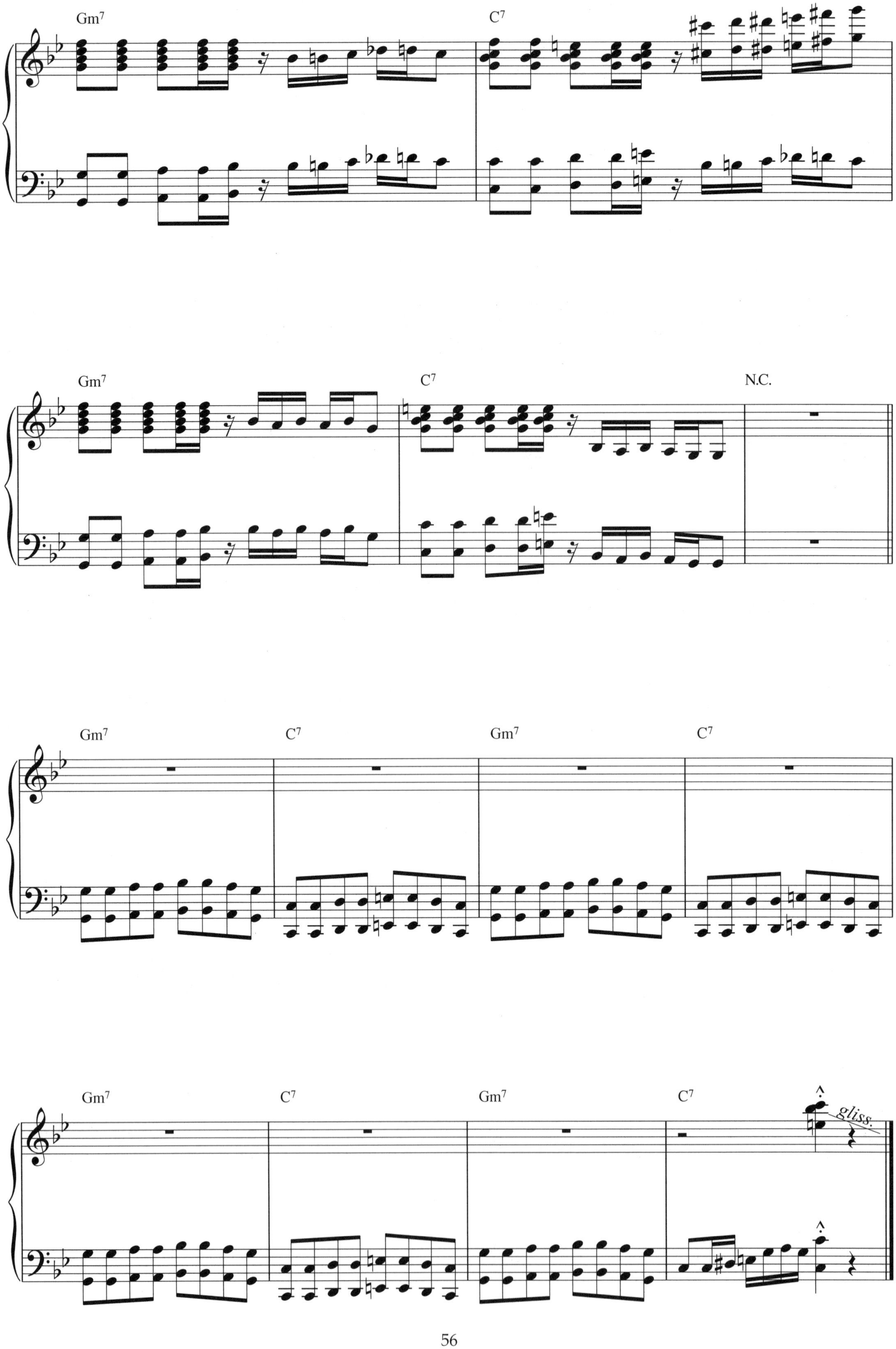
Gm7
C7
Gm7
C7
N.C.
Gm7
C7
Gm7
C7
Gm7
C7
Gm7
C7
gliss.

ANTONIO CARLOS JOBIM

Corcovado

(Quiet Nights Of Quiet Stars)

Words & Music by Antonio Carlos Jobim & Giorgio Calabrese

Am6
Abdim
Gm7
C7
Fmaj7
F6
Fm7
Em7
A7(b9)
D9
Dm7(b5)
G7
Am6
Abdim
Gm7
3

C7 Fmaj7 F6
Fm
mf
Fm(+7) Fm6
Em7
Am7
Dm7
G7
Em7(♭5)
A7(♭9)
Dm7
mp
G7 (♭5)
C
+9
A7+5
Dm7
N.C.
9
B♭6
9
C6
9
B♭6
9
C6
pp

Desafinado
(Slightly Out Of Tune)

ANTONIO CARLOS JOBIM

Words by Newton Mendonca
Music by Antonio Carlos Jobim

© Copyright 1959 IMG Songs UK (75%)/SACEM (25%).
All Rights Reserved. International Copyright Secured.

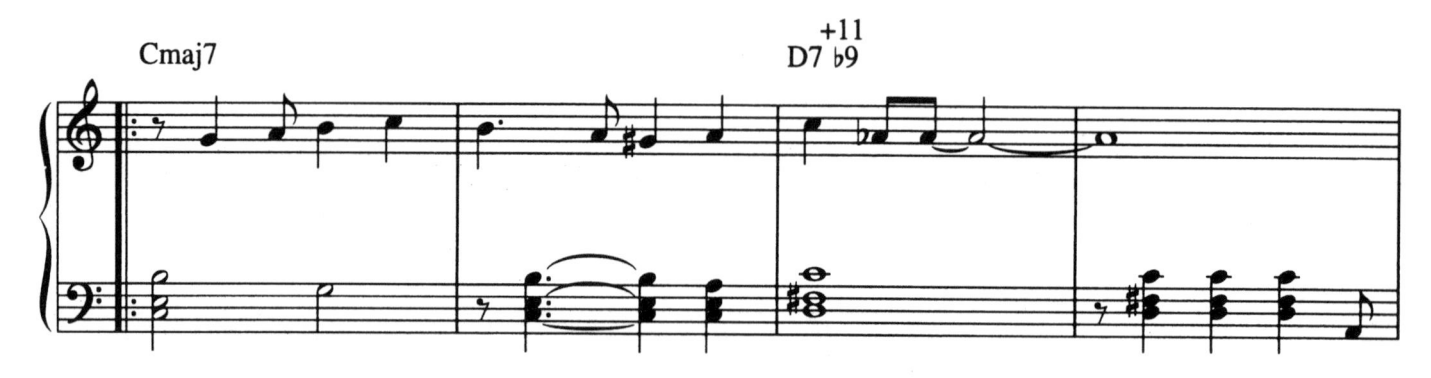

61

C♯m7
F♯m7
B7
Gmaj7
A♭dim
Am7
D7
Dm7
C♯dim
Dm7
G7
G7+9+5
Cmaj7
D7 +11 ♭9
Dm7
/G
G7
Em7♭5
A7
Dm7
B♭7

Cmaj7
Am7
D7
B♭9
D7
D♭maj7
D♭7
C6
F♯m7♭5
B7
Emaj7
Fdim
F♯m7
B7
F9
Emaj7
Fdim
F♯m7
B7
Emaj7

C♯m7
F♯m7
B7
Gmaj7
A♭dim
Am7
D7
Dm7
C♯dim
Dm7
G7
Cmaj7
D7 ♭9 +11
Dm7
/G
G7
Em7♭5

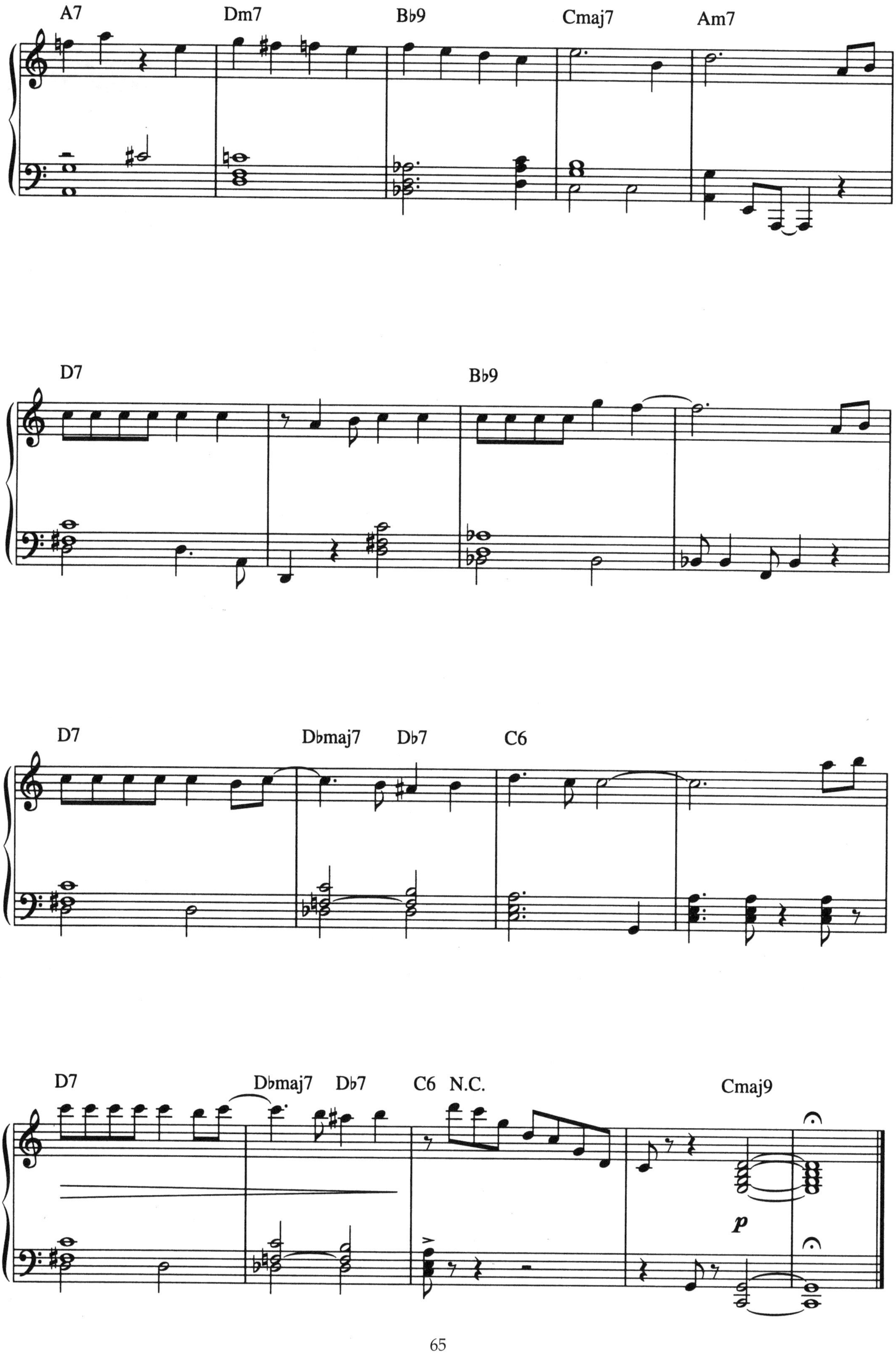
A7
Dm7
B♭9
Cmaj7
Am7
D7
B♭9
D7
D♭maj7
D♭7
C6
D7
D♭maj7
D♭7
C6
N.C.
Cmaj9
p

NORAH JONES
Don't Know Why

Words & Music by Jesse Harris

© Copyright 2002 Beanly Songs/Sony/ATV Songs LLC, USA.
Sony/ATV Music Publishing (UK) Limited.
All Rights Reserved. International Copyright Secured.

Gm7 C7 E♭/F B♭ B♭ma7 B♭7
E♭ Daug Gm7 C7 E♭/F B♭ Gm
mf
C13 F F7 Gm
C13 F F/E♭ Dm7 F/C
3
B♭ma7 B♭7 E♭ Daug Gm7 C7
mp

E♭/F B♭ B♭ma7 B♭7 E♭ Daug
3
Gm7 C7 E♭/F B♭ Gm C13
mf
F7 Gm
C13 F F6 F7
B♭ma7 B♭7 E♭ Daug Gm7 C7
mp

E♭/F B♭ B♭ma7 B♭7 E♭ Daug
Gm7 C7 E♭/F B♭ma7 B♭7
E♭ Daug Gm7 C7 E♭/F B♭
B♭ma7 B♭7 E♭ Daug Gm7 C7 E♭/F B♭
poco rall.
Gm7 C7 F7 B♭ Gm7 C7 E♭/F B♭
p

THELONIOUS MONK
Monk's Mood

Music by Thelonious Monk

© Copyright 1946 (Renewed 1973) Consolidated Music Publishing, a division of Music Sales Corporation & Embassy Music Corporation, USA.
Dorsey Brothers Music Limited.
All Rights Reserved. International Copyright Secured.

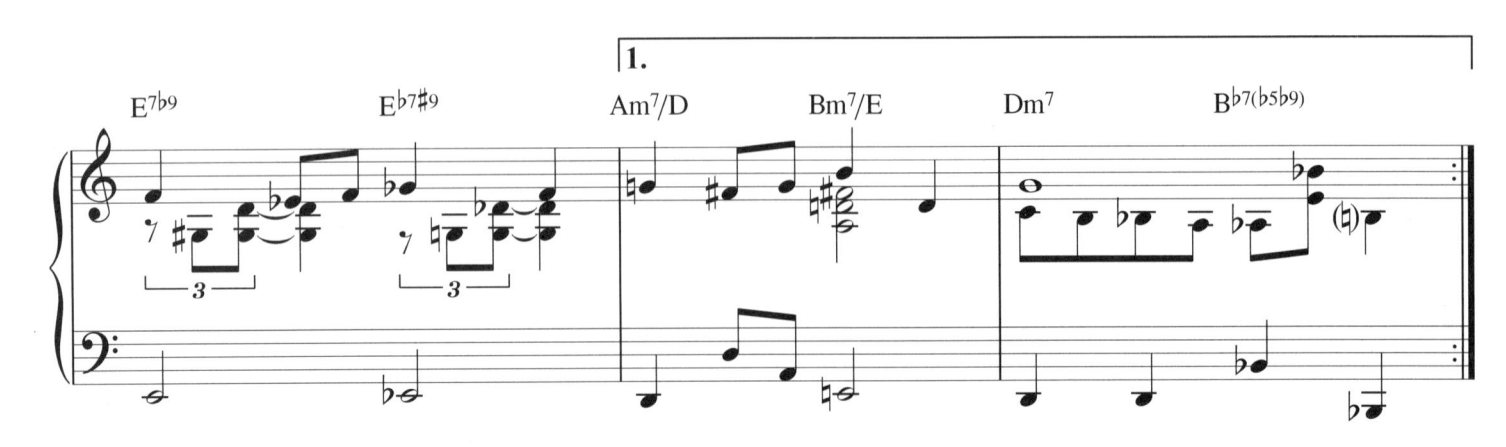

2.
A♭7♯5 G13 D♭maj7♭5 Gm7/C C7♭9
Gm7/C F♯m7 B7♭9 Emaj7
Am7♭5 A♭7 Dm7/G A♭dim7 Am7♭5 F7♯11
Fm7 E♭m7 Dm7 B♭7♭5 Fm7 B♭7♭5 Cmaj9
Dm7♭5 G7♭5 D♭maj7 C B

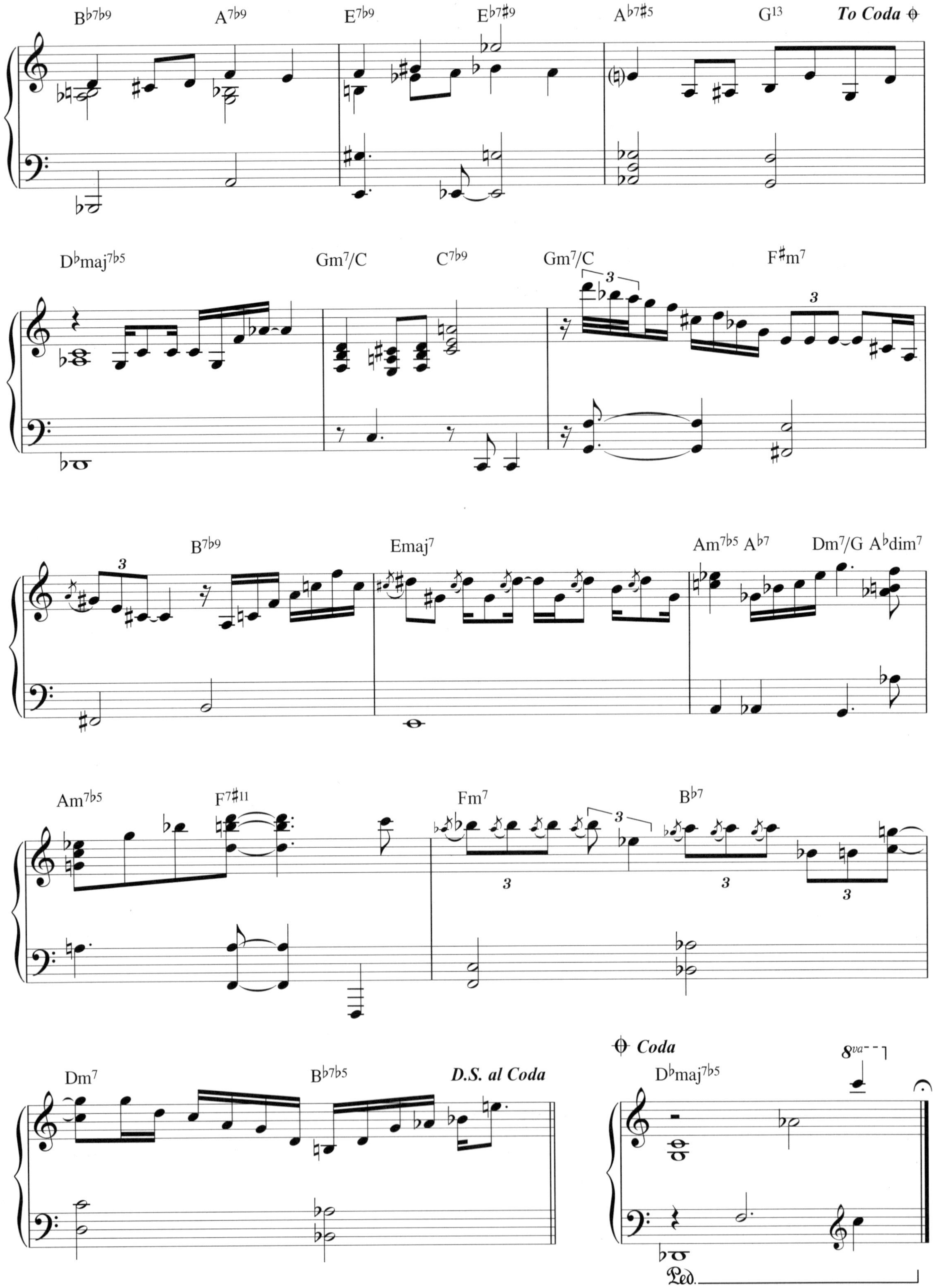
B♭7♭9
A7♭9
E7♭9
E♭7♯9
A♭7♯5
G13
To Coda
D♭maj7♭5
Gm7/C
C7♭9
Gm7/C
F♯m7
B7♭9
Emaj7
Am7♭5 A♭7
Dm7/G A♭dim7
Am7♭5
F7♯11
Fm7
B♭7
Dm7
B♭7♭5
D.S. al Coda
Coda
D♭maj7♭5
8va
Ped.

THELONIOUS MONK
Ruby, My Dear

Music by Thelonious Monk

Bbm11 A13 Bb7b5 Fm7 Bb7b9
3
Ebmaj7 Fm7 F#m7 Gm7 Ab6 A6 Gm7 C7b9 F7
Bbm7 Eb7b9 Abmaj7
8va
Bbm7 A13 Bm7 Bb7b5(b9) A7
3
3
Bm7 E7b9 Amaj13 Bb6 Bdim

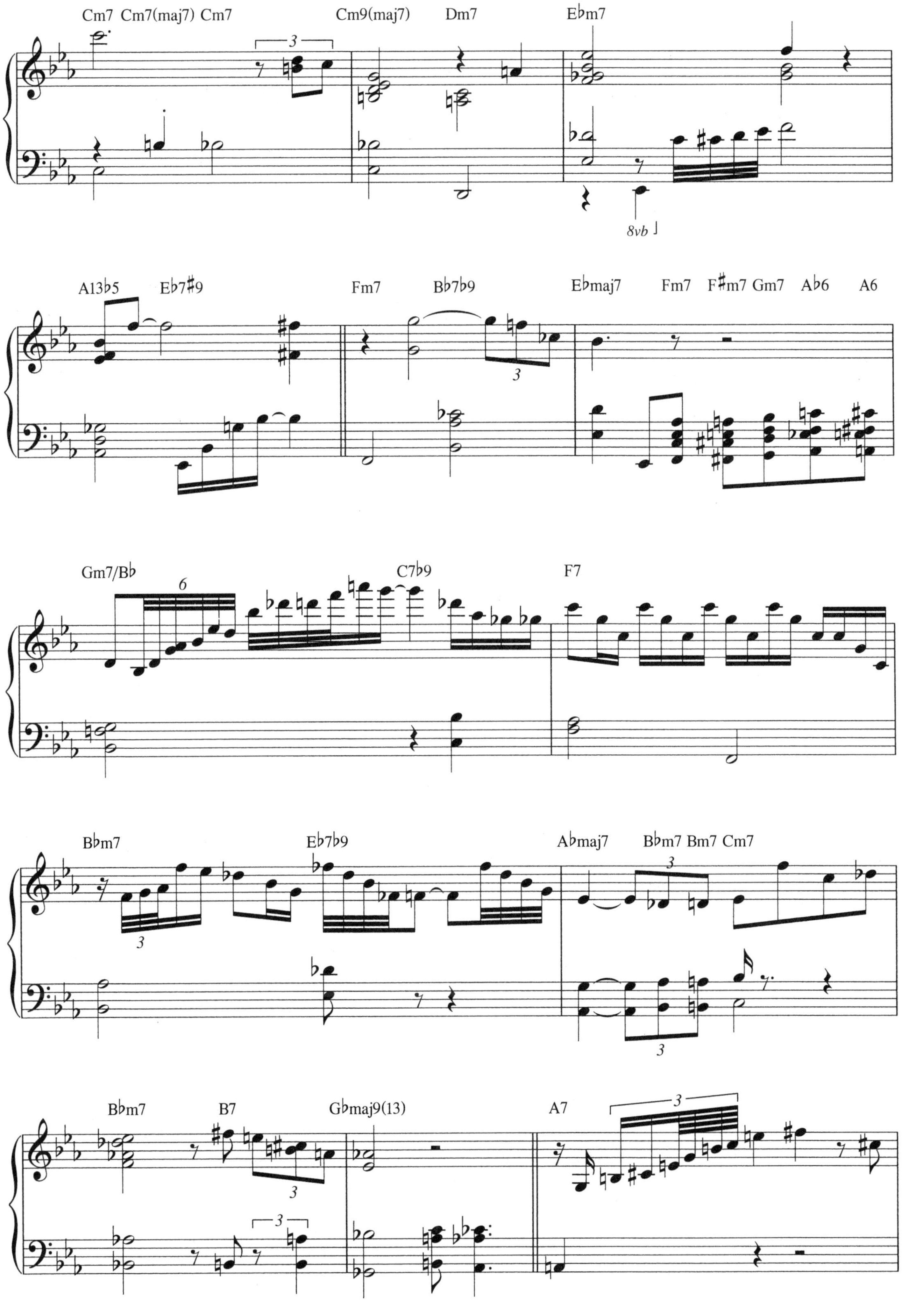
Cm7 Cm7(maj7) Cm7
Cm9(maj7)
Dm7
E♭m7
8vb
A13♭5
E♭7♯9
Fm7
B♭7♭9
E♭maj7
Fm7
F♯m7 Gm7
A♭6
A6
Gm7/B♭
C7♭9
F7
B♭m7
E♭7♭9
A♭maj7
B♭m7 Bm7 Cm7
B♭m7
B7
G♭maj9(13)
A7

Bm7
B♭7
A7
5
B♭
Bdim
Cm7 Cm7(maj7)
Cm7
3
Cm7
Dm7
E♭m7
A♭9♭5
E♭7♯9
Fm7
B♭7♭9
3
E♭maj7
Fm7
F♯m7
Gm7
A♭6
A6
Gm7/B♭
C7♭9
F7
3
8va
5

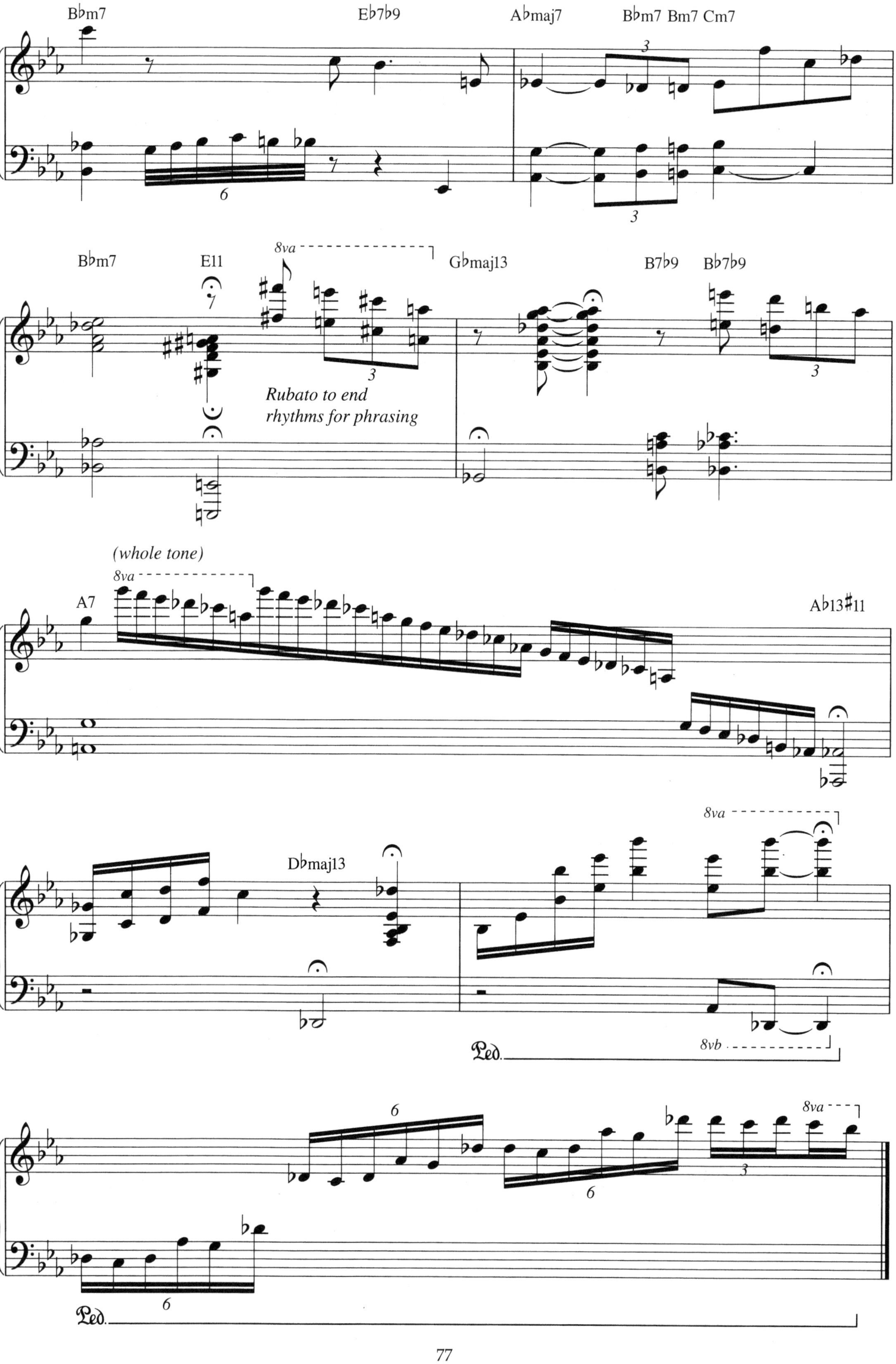
B♭m7
E♭7♭9
A♭maj7
B♭m7 Bm7 Cm7
E11
8va
G♭maj13
B7♭9
B♭7♭9
Rubato to end
rhythms for phrasing
(whole tone)
A7
A♭13♯11
D♭maj13
8vb

DUDLEY MOORE
Yesterdays

Words by Otto Harbach
Music by Jerome Kern

© Copyright 1933 Universal Music Publishing Limited (50%)/Chappell Music Limited (50%).
All rights in Germany administered by Universal Music Publ. GmbH.
All Rights Reserved. International Copyright Secured.

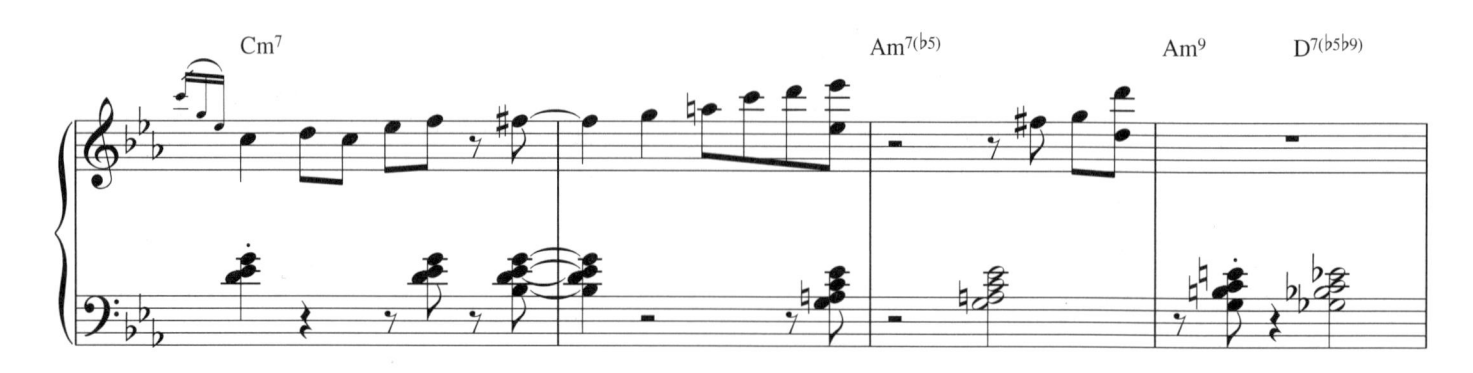

G7(♯9♭13)
Gm9
C7(♭9)
F9
Fm7
B♭13
B♭m9
E♭13
A♭maj9
Dm9
G7(♯9♭13)
Cm7
A♭7
G7(♭13)
Cm7
A♭7
G7(♭13)
Cm9
Am7(♭5)
Am7
D7(♭5♭9)
G7(♯9♭13)
To Coda
Gm9
C7(♭9)
F9
Fm9
B♭13
B♭m9
E♭13

A♭maj9
Dm9
G7(♯9♭13)
Cm7
Cm7
A♭7
G7(♭13)
Cm7
E♭9
A♭7
G7(♭13)
Cm7
F13
Am7(♭5)
Am9
D7(♭5♭9)
G7(♯9♭13)
Gm9
C7(♭9)
F9
Fm7
B♭9
B♭m9
E♭13

A♭maj9
Dm9
G7(♯9♭13)
Cm7
A♭9
G7(♭13)
Cm7
A♭maj7
A♭9
G7(♭13)
Cm7
Am7(♭5)
Am7
D7(♭5♭9)
G7(♭13)
Gm9
C7(♭9)
F9
Fm9
B♭13
B♭m9
E♭13
A♭maj9
Fm7
Dm9
G7(♯9♭13)

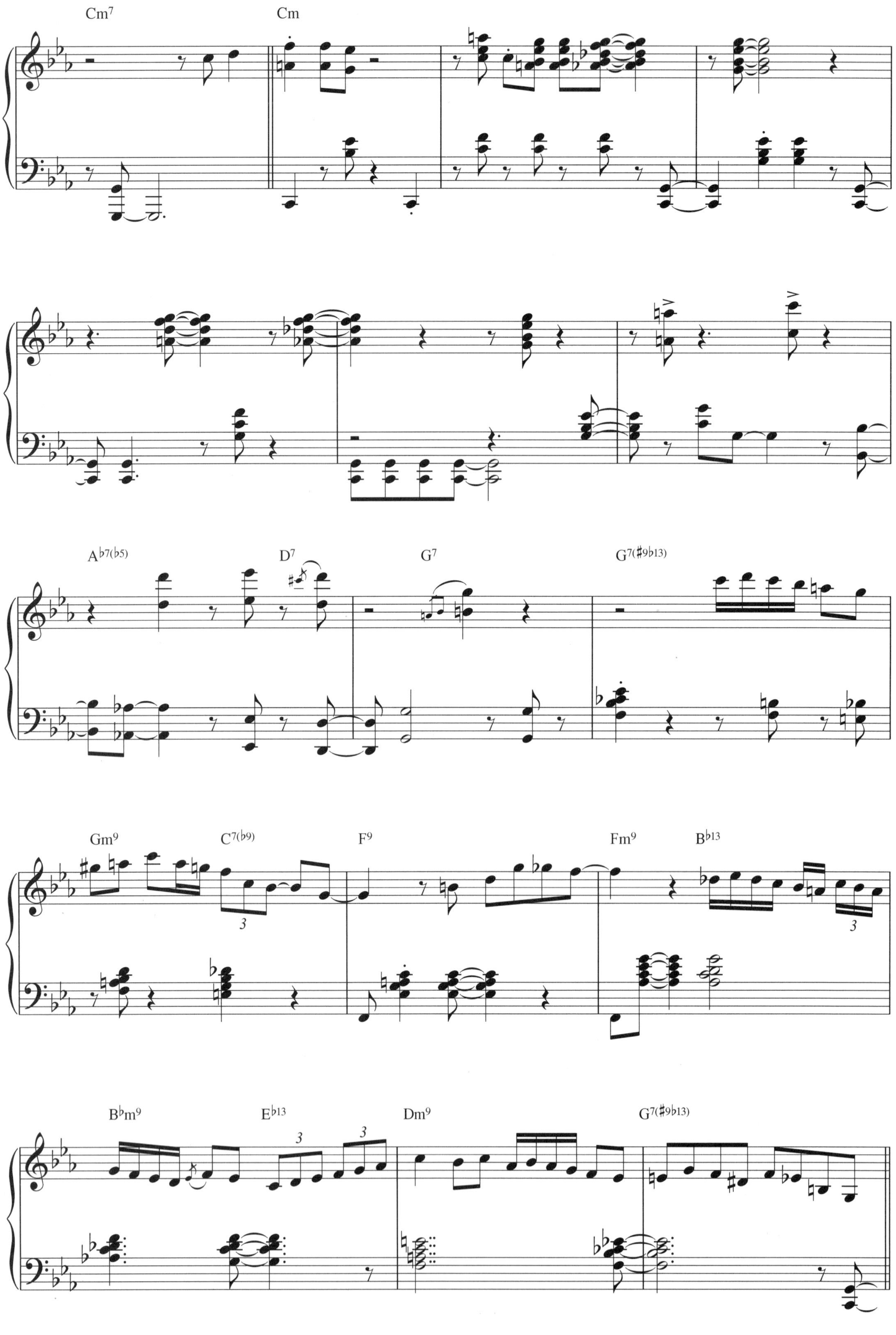
Cm7
Cm
A♭7(♭5)
D7
G7
G7(♯9♭13)
Gm9
C7(♭9)
F9
Fm9
B♭13
B♭m9
E♭13
Dm9
G7(♯9♭13)

Cm7
D♭/C
Cm7
D♭/C
Cm(ma7)
Cm7
Am7(♭5)
D7(♯9)
G7
Gm9
C7(♭9)
F9
Fm9
B♭13
B♭m9
E♭13
A♭maj7
Dm9
G7(♯9♭13)
Cm7
D.S. al Coda
Coda
molto rall.
B♭m9
E♭13
A♭maj9
Dm9
D♭13
A♭m9
Cm6(add 11)

GEORGE SHEARING
Lullaby Of Birdland

Words by George David Weiss
Music by George Shearing

© Copyright 1952, 1953 & 1954 Longitude Music Company, USA.
EMI Music Publishing (WP) Limited.
All Rights Reserved. International Copyright Secured.

Moderately with a beat

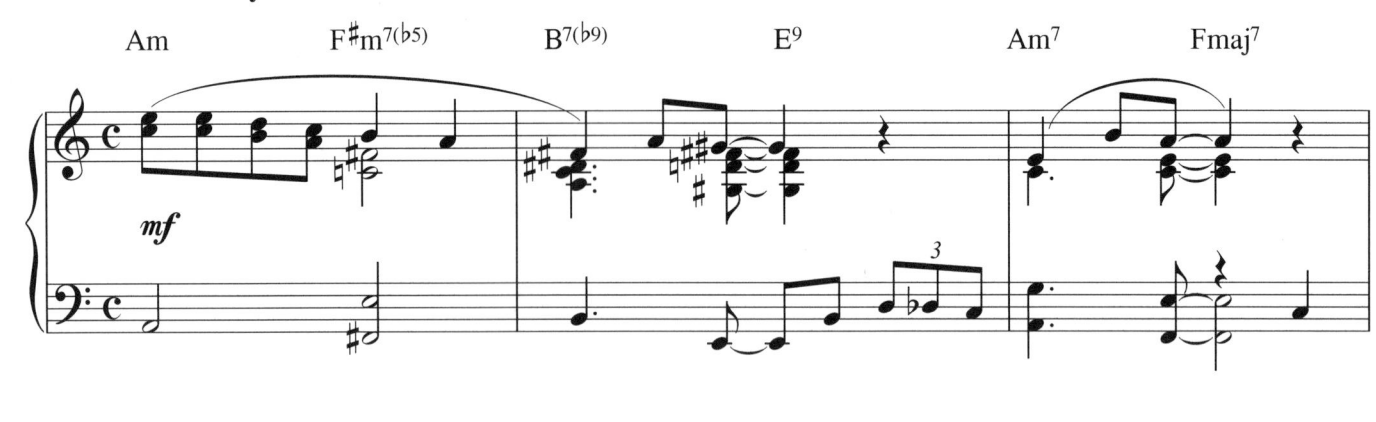

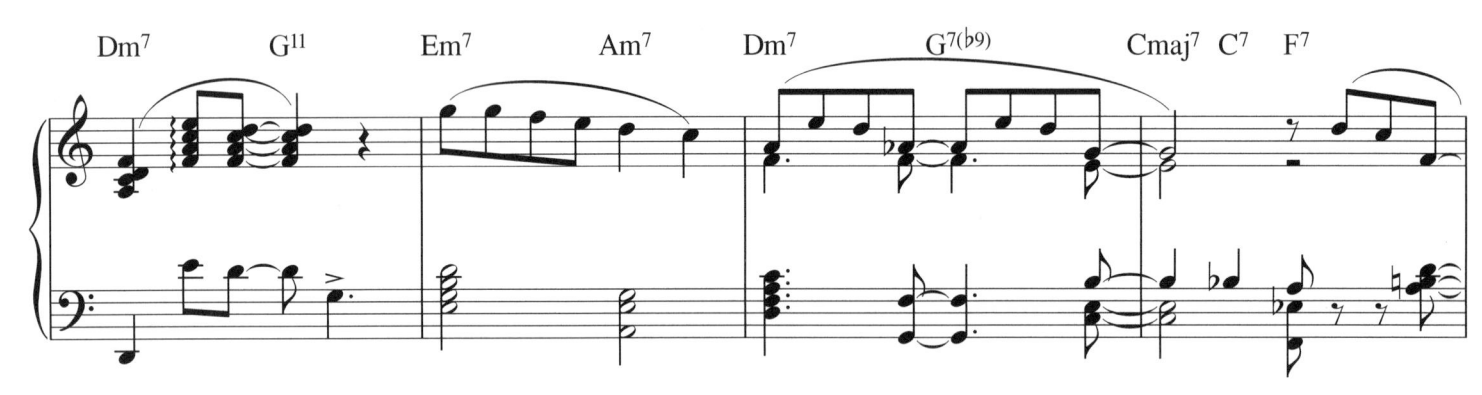

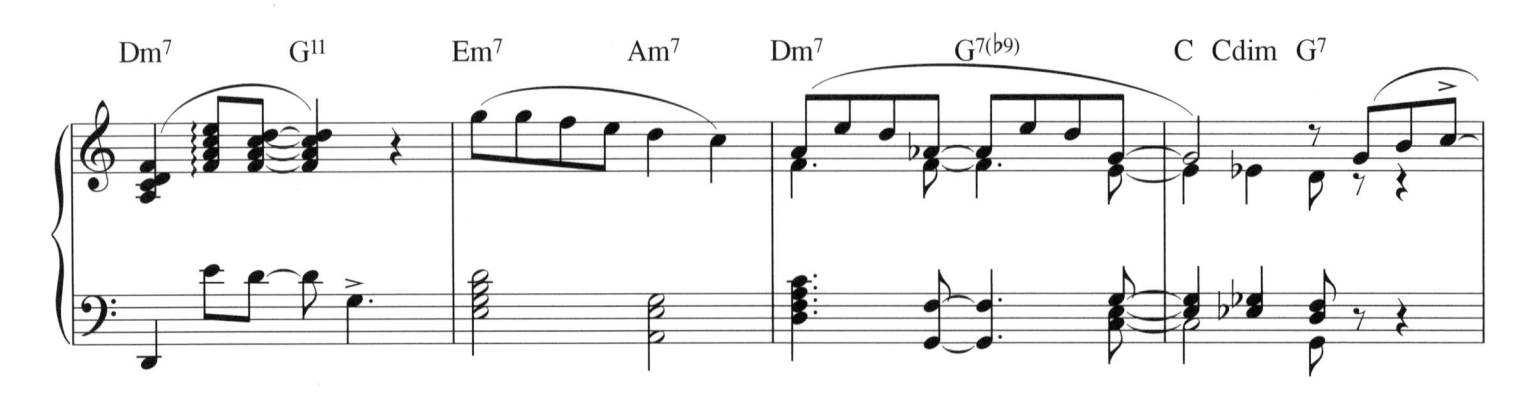

C
A7(♭9)
Dm7
G7(♭9)
Cmaj7 C7 C6 Caug5
A7(♭9)
Dm7
G7(♭9)
Cmaj7
E7
Am
F♯m7(♭5)
B7(♭9)
E9
Am7
Fmaj7
Dm7
G11
Em7
Am7
Dm7
G7(♭9)
Cmaj7 C7 F7
Bm7(♭5)
E7
Am
F♯m7(♭5)
B7(♭9)
E9
3
3

Am7 Fmaj7 Dm7 G9 Em7 Am7
Dm7 G7(♭9) Cmaj9 F7 Bm7(♭5) E7
mf
Am F♯m7(♭5) B7(♭9) E9 Am7 Fmaj7 C♯dim7 Dm7
G9 Em7 Am7 Dm7 G7(♭9)
C Cdim G7 N.C. A7(♭9)
f

Dm7 G7(♭9) Cmaj7 C6
A7(♭9) Dm7 G7(♭9)
Cmaj7 E7 Am F♯m7(♭5) B7(♭9) E9
Am7 Fmaj7 Dm7 G9 Em7 Am7
Dm7 G7(♭9) C6 Cdim G7 N.C. C9(♯11)
ff
p

THOMAS 'FATS' WALLER
Honeysuckle Rose

Words by Andy Razaf
Music by Thomas 'Fats' Waller

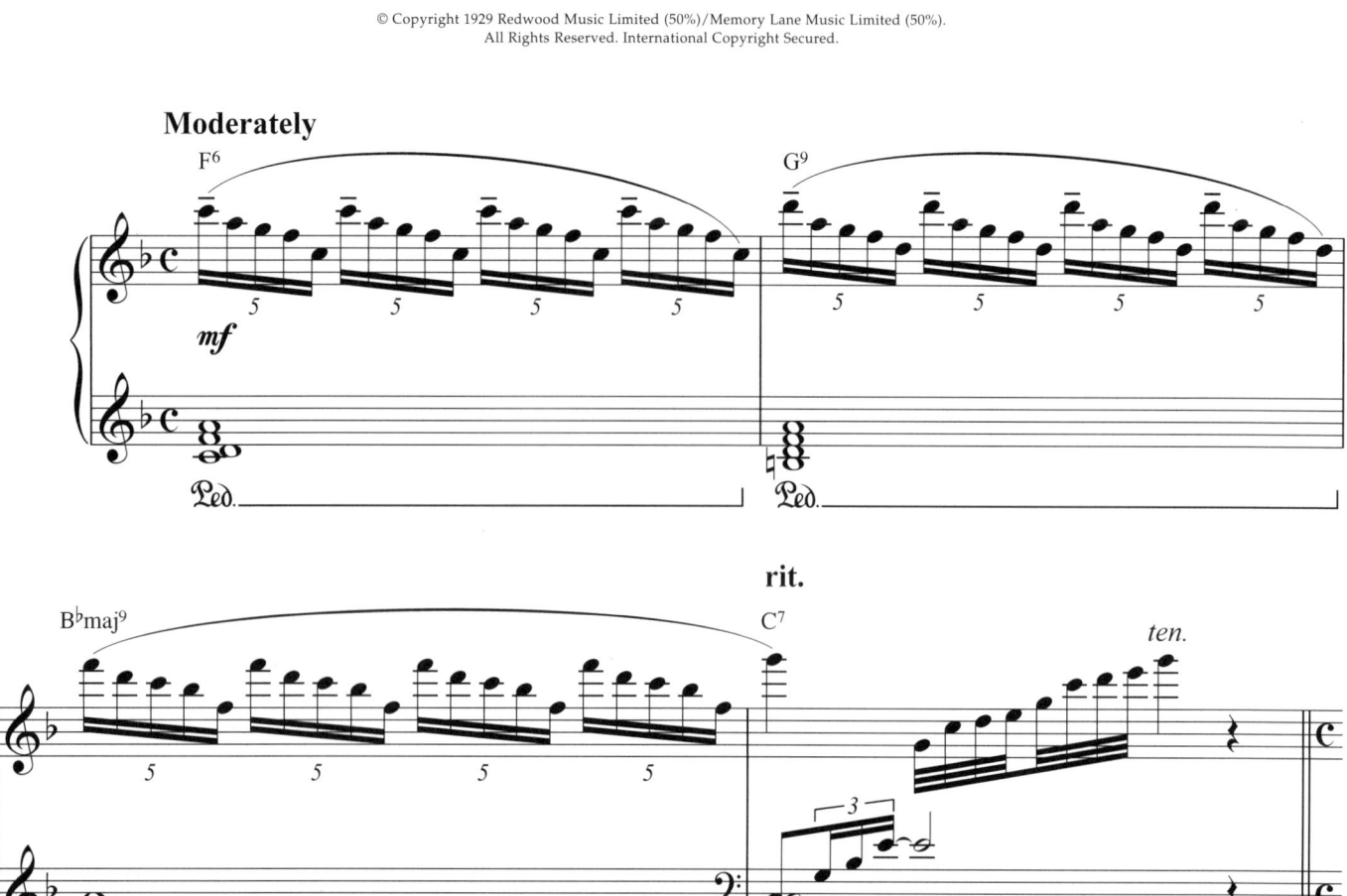

© Copyright 1929 Redwood Music Limited (50%)/Memory Lane Music Limited (50%).
All Rights Reserved. International Copyright Secured.

Dm7 G9 C Cdim7 C7 A♭dim7/C C7 A♭dim7
C7 D7(♭9) Gm G9 Gm7 C9
Ped. Ped.
Moderately slow
Gm7 C7 Gm7 C7 Gm7/C D♭9(♯5)
mf
C11 C9 N.C. F F7/A B♭ D♭/C♭ N.C.

F
C7/G
F/A
A♭dim7
Gm7
C9
Gm7
C9
Gm7
D♭9(♯5)
B♭/C
C9
N.C.
F
G♭maj7
G7
A♭6
Aaug5
B♭
C7
F
3
F7
B♭dim7/F
Bdim7/F
F7
B♭6
F7(♭9)
Edim7/F
B♭6/F

G7 Cdim7/G C♯dim7/G G7 Gm7/C
Ped.
C7(♯9) Gm7 C9 Gm7 B♭/C C9
Gm7 E♭9(♯11) D9 D♭9(♯5) C9 N.C. F F7/A
rit.
B♭ C9 F F7 B♭ Bdim7 F/C C7(♭13) F9

SCOTT JOPLIN
Maple Leaf Rag

Music by Scott Joplin

© Copyright 1906 Carlin Recorded Music Library Limited.
All Rights Reserved. International Copyright Secured.

E♭7
Bdim A♭/C
A♭ F7/A
E♭7
A♭ N.C.
F F/A B♭m
B♭9 E♭7
1. A♭ F7/A
2. A♭
A♭ Adim E♭7/B♭
(f)
A♭ Adim E♭7/B♭
E E♭
E E♭
A♭m
p
R.H.
L.H.

Ddim7
A♭/E♭
E
A♭/E♭
E♭7
A♭
mf
Ddim7
A♭/E♭
E
A♭/E♭
E♭7
A♭
Trio
A♭7/E♭
A♭7/G♭
A♭7/F
A♭7/E♭
D♭
D♭/A♭
D♭/F
D♭
B♭7/D
A♭7/E♭
A♭7/G♭
A♭7/F
A♭7/E♭
D♭
D♭/A♭
D♭/F
D♭
F7/C
B♭7
B♭7/D
B♭7/F
B♭7
E♭m
E♭m/G♭
E♭m
E♭m/G♭
Gdim7

1.
2.
D♭/A♭ B♭7 E♭9 A♭7 D♭ B♭7/D D♭ A♭7/C
D♭ Fm/C D♭ B♭m Bdim7 A♭/C A♭ F/A
E♭7/B♭ E♭7 F/A E♭7/B♭ E♭7 A♭ A♭/E♭ A♭ E♭7/B♭ A♭/C
D♭ Fm/C D♭ B♭m Bdim7 A♭/C A♭ A♭/E♭ D♭ B♭7(♭5) B♭7(♭5)/D
A♭/E♭ E7 B♭7/F E♭7/G A♭ E♭7/B♭ A♭/C A♭ E♭7 A♭
Fine

1 2 3 4 5 6 7 8 9

Bringing you the words and the music

All the latest music in print... rock & pop plus jazz, blues, country, classical and the best in West End show scores.

- Books to match your favourite CDs.

- Book-and-CD titles with high quality backing tracks for you to play along to. Now you can play guitar or piano with your favourite artist... or simply sing along!

- Audition songbooks with CD backing tracks for both male and female singers for all those with stars in their eyes.

- Can't read music? No problem, you can still play all the hits with our wide range of chord songbooks.

- Check out our range of instrumental tutorial titles, taking you from novice to expert in no time at all!

- Musical show scores include *The Phantom Of The Opera*, *Les Misérables*, *Mamma Mia* and many more hit productions.

- DVD master classes featuring the techniques of top artists.

Visit your local music shop or, in case of difficulty, contact the Marketing Department, Music Sales Limited, Newmarket Road, Bury St Edmunds, Suffolk, IP33 3YB, UK
marketing@musicsales.co.uk